THE HERITAGE STRATEGY
PLANNING HANDBOOK

THE HERITAGE STRATEGY PLANNING HANDBOOK

AN INTERNATIONAL PRIMER

by Marc Denhez

Dundurn Press
Toronto • Oxford

Editor: Wendy Thomas
Designers: Sebastian Vasile and Barry Jowett
Printer: Webcom

Canadian Cataloguing in Publication Data

Denhez, Marc, 1949–
      The heritage strategy planning handbook: an international primer

Companion vol. to: Legal and financial aspects of architectural conservation.

ISBN 1-55002-283-0

1. Historic buildings — Conservation and restoration — Planning.   2. Historic preservation — Planning.   I. Title

NA105.D46 1997   363.6'9   C97–930639–6

1   2   3   4   5   BJ   01   00   99   98   97

We acknowledge the support of the **Canada Council for the Arts** for our publishing program. We also acknowledge the support of the **Ontario Arts Council** and the **Book Publishing Industry Development Program** of the **Department of Canadian Heritage.**

THE CANADA COUNCIL | LE CONSEIL DES ARTS
FOR THE ARTS | DU CANADA
SINCE 1957 | DEPUIS 1957

Printed and bound in Canada.

 Printed on recycled paper.

Dundurn Press
8 Market Street
Second Floor
Toronto, Ontario, Canada
M5E 1M6

Dundurn Press
73 Lime Walk
Headington, Oxford
England
OX3 7AD

Dundurn Press
250 Sonwil Drive
Buffalo, NY
U.S.A. 14225

TABLE OF CONTENTS

PREFACE

How does a country design its strategy for the protection and rehabilitation of buildings?

This is a question which the international community has been addressing for over thirty years. The first major intergovernmental documents were UNESCO Recommendations: these were statements of intent, drafted at international expert meetings, approved (unanimously) by the governing body of the United Nations Educational, Scientific and Cultural Organization, and then submitted to the governments of the Member-States for their official consideration. Later, many of the same themes were revisited and expanded at an even higher level, namely at international meetings of States under the direct auspices of the U.N. General Assembly.

The importance of these proceedings is partly due to the moral authority of the assembled States. However, it is also due to the significant investment of time and effort whereby the international community has produced something of intrinsic value. These various documents and declarations represent a body of thought to assist Member-States in designing their strategy, and any government would be ill-served if it neglected to avail itself of these materials, if only for purposes of deliberation.

These documents were produced against a backdrop of governmental policy which dates back to antiquity. It was in the year 457 A.D. that the Roman emperor Majorian introduced the first known statute for the protection of major buildings. However, as recently as a generation ago, the relevant statutes of most countries were barely distinguishable from what Majorian had enacted 1500 years earlier. Almost unanimously, they relied upon a three-pronged framework, referred to as the "Three Pillars" in this writer's native Canada and under different titles elsewhere: overall strategy for the protection of buildings allegedly had the following components:

- **recognition** (*i.e.* a methodical and defensible system to distinguish properties "of interest" from those without interest);

- **protection** of properties of interest against infringement (presumably achieved by government veto on changes); and

- **financial support** for heritage properties to compensate for the "naturally" higher costs associated with them.

This was a logical outgrowth of heritage strategy in other countries which, for centuries, had grappled with the dilemma of "monuments", particularly those which had outlived their original function. However, few theories last forever, and the "Three Pillars" theory was no exception. To be specific,

- **recognition** (by the 1980s) was no longer viewed as a black-and-white categorization, but rather as "shades of grey", as an increasing number of expert meetings looked at the *entirety* of "the built environment": giving priority to specific buildings or areas would still be essential, but for pragmatic reasons, not philosophical ones.

- **Protection**, via public sector veto (on private sector activities) was no longer viewed as adequate because (a) the public sector was as guilty of threatening heritage as the private sector was, and (b) emphasis was shifting away from what *not* to do with heritage properties, toward what *should* be done with heritage properties.

- Under the influence of the *Report of the World Commission on Environment and Development* (1987) on the subject of "sustainable development", discussion of **financial support** was similarly shifting away from "incentives" to "the removal of *dis*incentives", on the premise that the "uncompetitive" position of heritage was more artificial than intrinsic, and could also be addressed by a variety of targeted corrective measures.

The evolution of tone and content in the international documents was also being accompanied by a rapid growth in the number of buildings under consideration. A generation ago, the general perception was that the focus would be on only a tiny minority. Although some rare countries (*e.g.* the United Kingdom) subjected over 8% of their buildings to heritage supervision, the typical pattern has been to focus on less than 5%. In the U.S.A., the conventional wisdom is that some 2-3% of all buildings would ever be considered eligible for the National Register of Historic Places. This was the logical consequence of a system in which *all* buildings were presumed expendable, *unless* some compelling reason could be advanced for different treatment. Indeed, it is arguable that it is that very presumption that made the Three Pillars approach necessary. That presumption was at the foundation of almost every policy system in the world, among capitalist and socialist countries alike. The philosophical underpinnings of that presumption, however, were shaken by the World Commission on Environment and Development (the Brundtland Commission). By the time that the international community held the "Earth Summit" in Rio de Janeiro in 1992, there were many voices saying that the presumption had been reversed: all investments (including buildings) are presumed re-usable, unless some compelling reason can be advanced otherwise.

That reversal of philosophical approach remains profoundly controversial, despite the international statements that emanated from Rio de Janeiro or the more recent (and germane) Habitat II Conference in Istanbul in 1996. Like all debates which were triggered by the international community's call for "sustainable development", the full ramifications are barely beginning to be felt, and are occasionally greeted not only with discomfort, but outright hostility.

The international heritage community has had its own difficulties in attempting to foresee where this paradigm shift would lead. At one expert meeting at the Université de Montréal in May 1996, it was argued

- that the subject of heritage could be viewed as a *range* of targets (from the very small to the very big, e.g. an entire national environment), and

- that there would therefore be a range of relevant values, strategies and tactics.

This theme of applying different approaches, depending on the targeted property's geographic scale, bears an uncanny resemblance to the recommendations which emanated from the Second United Nations Conference on Human Settlements (Habitat II) a month later.

The primary problem with these international documents, however, is accessibility. Advice concerning national strategy in this area is either spread over hundreds of pages (in the case of the UNESCO Recommendations), or scattered in discrete paragraphs interspersed with other subjects (in the case of the U.N. conferences). For any professional in this field, the task of working with these advisory documents has been daunting.

This is what led the undersigned to prepare this book. It is this writer's summary and categorization of the proposals from the international texts. By definition, any such summary or categorization represents a personal and subjective interpretation of those documents. Although this writer has attempted to remain faithful to the originals, there is no substitute for ultimate reference to the original texts. The primary source documents are the following:

- **Conventions and Recommendations of UNESCO concerning the protection of the cultural heritage,**[1]

- **Global Strategy for Shelter to the Year 2000,**[2]

- **Agenda 21,**[3]

- **The Habitat Agenda.**[4]

The most problematic area for heritage strategy, from all appearances, was to anticipate how the theories of "sustainable development" would ultimately affect heritage policy. There is a substantial body of opinion which holds that there will be no such effect at all, and that a country's heritage strategy in the future need not depart significantly from what had been anticipated a generation ago. With all possible respect, this writer cannot share that view. The international community has spoken repeatedly about the application of the principles of sustainable development across all areas of governmental strategy including buildings (as reflected at Habitat II). As complex as the subject is, a country must use its best efforts to deliberate on how this relationship is likely to play itself out in the realm of national strategy.

Positive and negative examples from some 20 jurisdictions are cited in this text. Some are drawn from my own experience with situations in Canada and elsewhere in the past 20 years, but many others came to my attention through the efforts of my colleagues in other countries. The vast majority of these examples are not "place specific": indeed, in most cases, both the problems and their solutions could occur in almost any country on earth.

It is hoped that this international profile will provide governments, planners, professionals and other stakeholders with a starting point for the drafting of their own national strategies. That is not to suggest that the strategy in any given country can or should necessarily correspond to international models in every case.

---

1 *Conventions and Recommendations of Unesco concerning the protection of the cultural heritage*, UNESCO, Paris, 1984

2 *The Global Strategy for Shelter to the Year 2000*, (adopted by the General Assembly of the United Nations at its 43rd Session, Resolution 43/181, 1988), published by the United Nations Centre for Human Settlements, Nairobi, 1990.

3 *Agenda 21* is the collection of recommendations flowing from the United Nations Conference on the Environment and Development (Rio de Janeiro, 1992) published in *The Earth Summit*, United Nations, New York, 1993.

4 *The Habitat Agenda* is the collection of recommendations flowing from the Second United Nations Conference on Human Settlements (Istanbul, 1996). It is available online at www.undp.org/un/habitat/agenda. At the time of writing this book, the official publication of *The Habitat Agenda* still awaited printing.

This is particularly true if a country proposes to "think strategically." A "strategy" is more than the sum of its parts; and it is certainly more than a collection of disparate pronouncements cobbled together from international precedents. To call something a "strategy" presupposes that a country has seriously reflected upon the goals that it pursues, the challenges that it must overcome, the systematized response to obstacles, the recruitment of national resources and stakeholders, and the sustainability of this initiative over the long term.[5]

It is arguable that most of the world's countries have neither an "existing building strategy" nor a "heritage strategy" which come even remotely close to meeting these criteria. That is part of the reason why the international community has worked so hard on the development of these advisory documents. However, before a country can develop a *"vision d'ensemble"* for the future of its buildings, the indispensable first step is for the country to take stock of its circumstances and to assess its own aspirations. One phrase which is repeated regularly in the international declarations, and which was not repeated in this book merely for reasons of space, is the all-important caveat that a given policy should be introduced "where appropriate". The first task is to ascertain when the international experience raises a *valid question*, worthy of further exploration within a given country.

If the following book succeeds only in raising such questions during the process of designing true national strategies, it will have amply served its purpose.

Marc Denhez
Ottawa, 1997

---

5 This objective is akin to what is called ITUC ("Integrated Territorial and Urban Conservation") by some heritage organizations, notably the International Centre for the Conservation and Restoration of Monuments (ICCROM); Rome. see *ITUC '97 Programme*, ICCROM, Rome '97.

1. DIFFERENT MODELS FOR COMMON OBJECTIVES

1.1 A Range of Models

Subject Matter

The subject of this book is buildings, particularly the protection and rehabilitation of those of architectural or historic interest. This topic has been referred to, using a variety of expressions:

Nomenclature

- Some countries (e.g. the U.S.A.) refer to it under the title "historic preservation" — even though buildings represent only one part of a country's "historic" artifacts.
- In England and Canada, such duties are assigned to agencies bearing the name "heritage" (e.g. English Heritage) — even though the word "heritage" is also applied to other kinds of property (e.g. landscapes) and activities (e.g. folklore).
- In other countries such as France, Germany and Italy, the relevant term focuses on "monuments" — even though "monuments" also include archaeological sites which, since UNESCO's New Delhi Recommendation (1956), have been targeted for distinct strategies and tactics.
- Finally, the last few years have witnessed the rise of the term "built environment" — even though this concept obviously has broader sweep than the ones above.

Although there are clear differences in emphasis (explored in this book), these expressions invariably relate to a country's policies toward some or all of its existing buildings. It is the collection of those policies — as a "national strategy" or otherwise — which will be discussed in this book, particularly as that strategy is reflected in a country's legislation.

A Variety of policy areas

Legislation with the single objective of protection and rehabilitation of buildings has stemmed from one or more of the following main policy areas (though not necessarily in the following order):

Housing

- conservation and upgrading of housing and neighbourhoods;

Heritage

- conservation and promotion of "heritage" buildings and districts;

Enviroment
Sustainability

- conservation of environment; and
- sustainable development, which the U.N's Agenda 21 defined as follows: "to ensure socially responsible economic development while protecting the resource base and the environment for the benefit of future generations."[1]

A variety of formats

Not surprisingly, although legislation for the protection and/or the rehabilitation of buildings is prevalent among most countries of the world, it does not follow a single model. Depending on the model chosen, the entire strategy of legislation within a given country could evolve dramatically differently from that of another. In some countries, the choice of model was intentional; in others, it was accidental. The result has been five families of statutes that are important for the protection of buildings:

SPECIES	DERIVATION
Statutes evolving from efforts to protect **artistic works**	These are the statutes that have the most self-conscious "cultural" orientation, and were historically the first set of protective statutes to be enacted. Their focus has been on the protection of individually identified artifacts, often labelled "monuments."
Statutes evolving from **archaeological legislation**	These statutes tended to confer protection not according to individual identification, but by genus (e.g., "earthworks").
Statutes evolving from **land-use controls**	These statutes evolved, in thrust and format, on the model of legislation pertaining to urban and regional planning and/or the protection of housing.
Statutes evolving from **environmental controls**	This legislation conferred protection according to concepts and mechanisms drawn from the protection of natural parks and, later, sites of natural/ecological significance or "the environment" generally.
Statutes in pursuit of **sustainable development**	This legislation has a different focus, namely to extend the utility and economic life of investments and materials.

1.2 Common Objectives

Controls and inducements

All forms of protective legislation for buildings have certain common challenges that they were designed to remedy. As with any other area of legislative activity, this legislation can be divided into three main categories:

- regulation by the State;
- inducements, with overt State participation; and
- adjustments to the general civil law affecting how citizens deal with each other.

Sectors

In turn, each of these categories can apply to either the public sector or the private sector.

Basic objectives

Expressed another way, after setting up its planning system,

- the public sector can control its own demolition/deterioration of buildings;

- the public sector can assess how its own activities can be an inducement to positive action in the built environment;

- the public sector can impose controls on the private sector;

- the public sector can introduce inducements for the private sector;

- legislation can create a climate for private individuals to sign positive contracts with one another (these private contracts can bear features that control behaviour and that provide a "consideration," i.e., a *quid pro quo* or inducement).

These objectives can be summarized as follows:

	STRATEGY AND PLANNING	
	CONTROLS	INDUCEMENTS
Public Sector Intervention	Controls on Public Sector	Public Sector Inducements
Overt Intervention in Private Sector	Controls on Private Sector	Inducements for Private Sector
Residual Influence and Facilitation in Private Sector	Private Contracts	

Authority
Finally, legislative intervention can take place at any of several possible levels — such as

- international law,
- the national level or
- the regional or municipal level.

Proposed international perspective
The following analysis begins with a profile of the international legal background. This is not merely because of the formal status or influence that international texts are supposed to have on a signatory State's legislation; it is primarily because many of the international texts represent the result of years of preparatory work and represent an accumulated expertise that is intrinsically helpful.

2. THE INTERNATIONAL STARTING POINT: TREATIES

2.1 Introduction

"In developing their national priorities, countries should take account of their international obligations."[2]

Agenda 21, adopted at the United Nations Conference on the Environment and Development, 1992.

The role of treaties
When a country undertakes a national legislative strategy on a given subject, the components of that strategy may, in part, be already predetermined. This is the case, for example, where a country has already signed a binding international agreement to include certain measures in its legislation. International treaties can have that effect. At present, there are important multilateral treaties on the subjects of housing and of heritage, but not yet on that of sustainable development.

2.2 Treaties on Housing

The United Nations has been deeply involved with the question of housing. This involvement stems from the International Covenant on Economic, Social and Cultural Rights (CESCR), which recognizes the right of everyone to an adequate standard of living … including … housing, and the continuous improvement of living conditions.

The application of this treaty obligation to the protection and rehabilitation of buildings was interpreted in international declarations mentioned later in this report.

2.3 Treaties on "Heritage"

Hague
Convention

There are two principal international treaties dealing with that component of the built environment that can be called of "heritage" value. The first is the Hague Convention of 1954[3] which focuses on the protection of historic monuments in times of armed conflict.[4]

World Heritage
Convention

In the second, the World Heritage Convention,[5] the "heritage" referred to includes both the natural heritage and the immovable cultural heritage (e.g., buildings and archaeological sites). The Convention imposes upon each Member-State a

Basic duty

duty … of ensuring the identification, protection, conservation, presentation and transmission to future generations of the cultural and natural heritage … It will do all it can to do this and, to the utmost of its own resources …[6]

This includes the formal obligation

Measures

to take the appropriate legal, scientific, technical, administrative and financial measures for the identification, protection, conservation, presentation and rehabilitation of this heritage.[7]

Planning

From the standpoint of urban planning legislation, the Convention is even more specific. It establishes a formal obligation

- "to adopt a general policy which aims to give the cultural and natural heritage a function in the life of the community";[8] and
- "to integrate the protection of that heritage into com-

prehensive planning programs."[9]

Scope   Although the Convention confines this duty to sites of "outstanding universal value,"[10] it is up to each Member-State to determine how those properties will be defined.[11]

3. SEMI-OFFICIAL DOCUMENTS: THE INTERNATIONAL "DECLARATIONS" AND "RECOMMENDATIONS"

3.1 Introduction

Status of declarations   There are international documents that, without having the status of conventions or treaties, nevertheless have a certain amount of legal weight because they are signed by States in their sovereign capacity. One example is a resolution of the General Assembly of the United Nations on a subject like housing[12] or environment:[13] although such resolutions do not have the same legal binding effect as treaties, they nonetheless carry substantial weight in expressing the will of the international community. The weight to be attached to other international "declarations" depends on the official status of the group that made the declaration.

Lower-level perspectives   The following provides a more specific illustration. On one hand, there is the case of the four international symposia, *Urban Renewal and the Quality of Life*, under the auspices of the United Nations.[14] These symposia adopted formal conclusions and recommendations that are precisely on the subject of the conservation and rehabilitation of downtown districts (from a wide variety of perspectives including housing, urban planning, transportation, etc.). However, the number of participating countries[15] did not represent a true international cross-section, and the participants did not sign as heads of governments (or their representatives).

High-level conferences   At the opposite end of the spectrum, there is the United Nations Conference on Environment and Development (also known as UNCED, the Earth Summit, or the Rio Conference).[16]

- This conference was held on the authority of U.N. General Assembly Resolution 44-228[17]; and
- the conference's conclusions obtained the signatures of more heads of State than any other single document in world history up to that date.

3.2 Declarations on Sustainable Development

Agenda 21

The outcome of the Earth Summit was articulated in two relevant documents, namely the *Rio Declaration on Environment and Development* and *Agenda 21*. They represent the foremost statement of the international community on the subject of sustainable development and the moral obligations of signatory States. In response, the U.N. General Assembly established the United Nations Commission on Sustainable Development. The *Rio Declaration* constitutes a collection of statements of general principle, while the specific recommendations are outlined (in considerable detail) in *Agenda 21*. This attention to detail is equally clear in the sections pertaining to "sustainable human settlement development," covering buildings, neighbourhoods and cities. For example, *Agenda 21* specifies that countries should encourage local participation in "the protection and/or rehabilitation of older buildings."[18]

The subject of human settlements takes up a full chapter of *Agenda 21* and will be described later.

3.3 Declarations on Housing

Relevant U.N. declarations on housing began with the U.N. Conference on the Human Environment (1972) followed by the *Vancouver Declaration on Human Settlements* (Habitat 1976).[19] A large part of the motivation stems from the fact that over 1 billion people in the world live in inadequate housing, and over 100 million people are essentially homeless. In view of this scarcity of adequate housing, the General Assembly has endorsed a series of statements, most notably the *Global Strategy for Shelter to The Year 2000*,[20] adopted by resolution of the General Assembly in 1988.[21] The following has been described as a cornerstone:[22]

> All citizens of all States, poor as they may be, have a right to expect their Governments to be concerned about their shelter needs, and to accept a fundamental obligation to protect and improve houses in neighbourhoods, rather than damage or destroy them.[23]

The relevance of the *Global Strategy* to the specific subject of the protection and rehabilitation of buildings is further illustrated by the following direct quotations:

- "The bulk of the housing stock is already in place and a considerable effort is required to maintain it and gradually to improve it. The existing stock represents a capital asset."[24]
- "It is essential, in formulating shelter strategies, to consider carefully the role to be played by gradual shelter improvement vis-à-vis new construction."[25]
- Governments should "set objectives...for the upgrading and maintenance of the existing housing stock in terms both of the scale of the activity and of the housing standards to be met."[26]

Further recommendations are described later.

3.4 Declarations on Heritage

UNESCO Recommendations

International treaties on the subject of heritage have been supplemented by international "Recommendations."[27] These proposals were drafted from time to time by meetings of experts convened by the United Nations Educational Scientific and Cultural Organization (UNESCO) over a period of some thirty years. They covered topics as diverse as archaeological licensing and the loan structures that would be desirable in historic districts.

Status under UNESCO Treat

Each set of proposals was then submitted to the General Conference of UNESCO for ratification and typically adopted unanimously as a "UNESCO Recommendation."

Under the terms of UNESCO's own treaty and the adherence of Member-States to UNESCO, the standard protocol is then for the Recommendations to be distributed to the Member-States of UNESCO for comment on proposed implementation.

This dissemination is undertaken under the authority of another treaty, namely the one that established UNESCO and its constitution.[28]

Although each country voted for these Recommendations, which outline the contents of proper heritage legislation, the Recommendations (unlike the treaties) are not binding. However, insofar as they are part of a process entrenched in a treaty, they are expected to have some intangible legal status to "influence the development of national laws and practices"[29] so as to "apply the principles and norms aforesaid within their respective territories."[30]

3.5 Unofficial Documents

Non-legal opinions and "charters"

Certain non-governmental organizations such as the International Council of Monuments and Sites (ICOMOS)[31] have disseminated their own opinion of standards of good behaviour pertaining to heritage properties, under legal-sounding names. For example, ICOMOS has publicized its document called the Venice Charter.[32] However, as influential and thought-provoking as these documents may be, they have no intrinsic legal status, nor do they have a semi-official status comparable to, say, the UNESCO Recommendations.

4. THE INTERNATIONAL CHECKLIST

4.1 Declarations Summarized

The various declarations themselves occupy hundreds of pages, but can be summarized as follows (not an exhaustive list). The various declarations do specify that in several countries, the planning/regulatory process may be complicated by various factors (e.g., a federal system), so the following description is necessarily a simplification and is strictly unofficial. Anyone wishing to make formal use of these documents would presumably refer to the original, lengthier wording.

Recommendations (Abridged)	Commentary
Planning	
"Governments ... should adopt a national strategy for sustainable development based...on the implementation...of decisions particularly of *Agenda 21*."[33] They should also have official policies on shelter[34] and heritage.[35]	In most countries, this process has already begun. Governments have indeed established a national reporting structure and have started filing reports on how their national strategy contributes to sustainable development and the items on *Agenda 21*.
Planning has to be "cross-sectoral".[36] Social, economic, developmental, ecological and environmental data should be used simultaneously. The planning process should "stress interactions and synergisms."[37]	Although this point is repeated several times in international declarations, it appears difficult to implement. Many observers still complain that so few officials working in housing, sustainable development or heritage speak to each other that they do not even realize where their goals overlap. As such, they not only fail to plan together; they cannot even help each other, and this is counterproductive to the national interest.
There should be "sustainable development indicators" in national economic and social planning and decision-making practices.[38]	
Governmental policy development and protection should have direct input from non-governmental organizations.[39]	This is a theme that reappears frequently in international declarations.
The progress towards sustainable development should be reviewed "by the various sectors and departments of government" annually.[40]	This process has already begun, and many countries have already published their initial reports on their own specific follow-up to *Agenda 21*.
Shelter policy must be seen as an outgrowth of "fiscal, monetary and trade policies" and decision makers for shelter should "have a seat at the table of macro-economic planners."[41]	This challenging objective is again consistent with other U.N. recommendations.
All official plans (national, regional, local) must provide for heritage conservation.[42] Objectives pertaining to heritage property should be integrated into standard planning and land-use practices.[43]	This assumes that the country — or its regions or municipalities — have officially written plans that have specific legal effects. For example, the British Civic Amenities Act of 1967 created a legal obligation, on the part of munici-

Recommendations (Abridged)	Commentary
	palities, to plan for heritage buildings (or buildings potentially considered heritage) within their territory. At the opposite end of the governmental hierarchy, Greece entrenched the protection of major heritage sites in its constitution. Paradoxically, many countries that oblige their municipalities to plan for heritage omit to create a similar duty at the national level, and other countries that profess a national commitment omit to create a similar duty on the part of their local governments.
Alertness to heritage should extend to research and measures covering the entire area of the jurisdiction, not just predetermined sites.	
Governmental inventories of heritage should include both sites that have been designated for protection and those that have not.[44]	Many countries have systems where sites "of interest" are on a list, without having been designated for protection yet. In some countries (e.g., France), there is a further category of properties that, without yet enjoying full legal protection, are in an intermediate category where the owner must provide notice to the State of impending work.
Every government should have a body empowered to advise it on all heritage property endangered by projects by either the public sector[45] or the private sector.[46]	Although most countries have "co-ordinating" heritage agencies, the extent of real power varies dramatically. In many cases, the most resistance comes from other government departments, particularly tax authorities whose rules may be directly damaging to the economics of heritage buildings. Since many countries do not allow government agencies to sue each other, heritage agencies often cannot influence certain other government departments, even when they have legislation that appears to give them authority.
A public authority should be established to co-ordinate all activities affecting heritage property.[47]	

Recommendations (Abridged)	Commentary
Proposals for historic districts should make provision for local input.[48]	This is not only an expression of democratic principle — it is pragmatism (otherwise, the plans often fail).
The applicable rules should be codified.[49]	This refers primarily to an unofficial consolidation of relevant statutory provisions. It is not suggested that all the important provisions affecting heritage would be inscribed in a single statute; this is probably impossible — and even if it were possible, would probably be undesirable.[50]
Controls on the Public Sector	
Protective measures must be as binding on the public sector as on the private sector.[51]	Traditionally, this objective has been very difficult. Government officials were being placed in a conflict of interest, where the protection of heritage sometimes meant that they would have to oppose more powerful departments of the same government. A major breakthrough in many countries was to adopt the model of "impact assessments" under environmental legislation.
In areas of potential interest, any decision on construction should be preceded by a study of the various alternatives.[52]	S.106 of the U.S. National Historic Preservation Act of 1966 is one of the best-known examples of this approach. This (and related legislation) allows court applications that block projects where study has been inadequate.
Heritage designations should be binding on other government agencies, where public works should require authorization by the protective authorities.[53]	
Environmental impact procedures should not apply merely to individual projects, but "extend beyond the project level to (entire) policies and programs."[54]	This recommendation would mean that "environmental impact assessments" would apply not only to specific concrete projects, but should be done for entire systemic programs (e.g., certain loan programs, subsidy systems, etc.). This has made some government agencies nervous, particularly those that are administering programs that have a debatable long-term effect on sustainable development.

Recommendations (Abridged)	Commentary
Inducements Connected to Public Sector Buildings	
Uses should be found for heritage properties, to integrate them with present and future community needs. Governments should commit themselves to a policy for this purpose.[55]	Around the world, governments have often been more reluctant occupants of heritage buildings than the private sector. Inspired by Brasilia and Islamabad, many bureaucracies have waged campaigns to locate in the newest buildings. The U.S. Public Buildings Cooperative Uses Act of 1974 attempted to restrict this pattern, by forcing agencies to locate in government heritage buildings before looking elsewhere, but this law had no enforcement.
Public agencies should orient their own construction budgets to renovating space in heritage buildings.[56]	Ironically, many governments do the reverse.[57] It is not uncommon for school budgets or hospital budgets to have a higher percentage of State subsidy for the replacement of a building than for the rehabilitation of the same building.
Strict controls should be imposed upon subsidies to public housing projects that demolish buildings, and every effort should be made to use renovation instead as an instrument of public housing policy.[58]	The Netherlands has had one of the more successful programs to integrate the restoration of heritage buildings with its larger housing policy.
All levels of government, including municipalities, should be obliged to have a heritage service. These agencies should have direct access to governmental services and expertise at the higher government levels.[59]	Often, the statutory mandate of the national heritage agency does not include delivering advice to other government agencies on the most cost-effective techniques for intelligent restoration, so those other agencies often get the impression that restoration is too expensive. This mistake can be very costly.
Controls on the Private Sector	
Protection implies a ban on destruction or alteration, unless government consent is granted.[60]	This point has been repeated so often that many countries assume (mistakenly) that this is the only feature to heritage legislation.

Recommendations (Abridged)	Commentary
Landscapes should also be subject to protection, e.g., concerning cutting of trees, subdividing the property, etc.[61] No compensation should be payable for this.[62]	For example, historic gardens and landscapes are specifically covered in the legislation of several countries.
There should be a procedure for public notice and official registration for heritage designations.[63]	Some governments even arrange for newspaper notices of prospective heritage designations. Typically, protective legislation for a property is mentioned in the description of that property, at the local Land Titles office.
Within heritage districts, there should be a legal obligation to maintain properties.[64]	In many statutes (e.g., Québec's), the obligation to maintain is applied to all protected heritage properties, not only ones in districts. This is to avoid what the United States calls DBN ("Demolition By Neglect").
The area around heritage sites should be subject to rules ensuring harmonization.[65]	In some countries (e.g., France), the statute creates an automatic protected zone, to a specified radius around the property.
Groupings of modest buildings that are collectively of cultural interest should be protected even if no individual one is noteworthy.[66]	This is the foundation for many historic districts.
There should be special rules for signage in heritage areas.[67]	Rules concerning signage are customary components of heritage statutes.
Standard maintenance should not require authorization.[68]	Usually, the expression "alteration" (for the purposes of acquiring a governmental permit) is defined so that it does not include ordinary maintenance.
It should be possible to issue temporary stop orders.[69]	These temporary stop orders are emergency measures of protection, to stop destruction that might not otherwise be covered by the standard heritage process.
Individuals and groups must be given ways to become involved in the development and enforcement of laws for sustainable development.[70]	Although international declarations often refer to the role of community groups in the development of laws, this recommendation remains controversial among some government agencies. The question of enforcement is even more controversial. For example, although U.S. citizens usually have a

Recommendations (Abridged)	Commentary
	right[71] to apply to the courts to stop illegal activities, many other countries declare that only the government can apply to the courts in such cases (this places the government in a conflict of interest, if the law is being broken by another government agency).
Governmental powers should include the power of expropriation.[72]	This is usually considered a last resort, particularly where governments have to pay the fair market value and have little cash at their disposal to do so.
Offences should be punishable by significant sanctions, including the restoration of the property at the violator's expense.[73]	Some developers have told the media that they consider these fines to be merely a "cost of doing business." In some countries, these "costs" are even tax-deductible.
Appeal procedures should be foreseen.[74]	The intent of the Recommendation was for the appeal to go to a knowledgeable, impartial party, but instead, some legislation accidentally sends appeals to a normal judge instead, who must rule on the historic authenticity of an item (for which judges are not professionally trained). This unsatisfactory situation results from the "objective test trap" described later in this paper. In other places, the appeal is sometimes to political authorities, which can also cause some unsatisfactory situations.
Inducements for the Private Sector	
There may be a *quid pro quo* for designation.[75]	In many areas, there is comprehensive protective legislation, which officials refuse to use, because they see no viable future for the building. Politically, the future of heritage buildings is more secure when there is an economic plan for their re-use.
Any policy for protection must be accompanied by a policy for revitalization.[76]	

Recommendations (Abridged)	Commentary
Compatibility with sustainable development must be entrenched in "fiscal measures and the budget."[77]	This goal is extremely difficult to meet. In many countries, the tax authorities are at least *primus inter pares* among government departments; they do not feel themselves morally bound by the wishes of other ministries (such as housing, environment, culture), nor for that matter, by the diplomats who sign international declarations on behalf of the State. Some will declare openly that it is part of their job to refuse the "erosion of the tax base" routinely suggested by other government officials. The international declarations have nevertheless repeated the importance of this approach, in view of the decisive role that taxation can have in so many decisions.
Governments should support independent institutions (organizations and research institutes) to research "the role of environmental taxation."[78]	
Proprietors of heritage buildings (or in heritage districts) should be encouraged via tax incentives or the like.[79]	This is controversial. Although supporters of old buildings would all like to improve their economics, some prefer grants or subsidies specifically targeted to landmarks, while others support low-profile measures assisting restoration generally.
Governments should establish either special subsidies or a national preservation fund outside the normal budgetary process.[80]	
Governments should make grants, subsidies or loans available to municipalities, institutions and owners, to bring the use of heritage buildings up to contemporary standards.[81]	Ironically, many countries have a reverse problem: their lending institutions (even State banks) often have policies that are more unfavourable to designated heritage buildings than to other buildings (on the assumption, for example, that the bank would prefer to retain the option to destroy the property, if it took it over after default on a loan). Other countries have had prob-

Recommendations (Abridged)	Commentary
	lems because financial institutions would not lend to buildings where owners had trouble getting insurance (for example, in historic districts with higher-than-normal fire risks).
The loan system can be established, with public sector and private sector participation, to provide loans for rehabilitation, with low interest and/or long repayment schedules.[82]	
Governments should provide enterprises with "advice and assistance with information."[83] For example, governments should establish systems that offer "cost-effective solutions (and)...technological innovation"[84] — for example, on the use of traditional indigenous materials.[85] Forms of association should be developed, so that large firms can share information and technology with smaller firms.	Most governmental systems tell citizens what they should not do with their property; very few provide helpful guidance on what citizens should do. In the case of older buildings, this presents a serious problem, since many owners simply lack the knowledge to deal with those buildings effectively. The same problem extends to many renovation enterprises; use of the wrong technological approach can be not only more expensive, but may even threaten the building itself.
Red tape can be reduced for good projects. "Existing regulatory instruments often pose barriers to the delivery of shelter....They incorporate unaffordable construction techniques....They sometimes prohibit the use of traditional materials and techniques."[86]	This widespread complaint of entrepreneurs in rehabilitation in many countries addresses the problem of construction standards that were drafted exclusively with new buildings in mind.
Countries should promote "culturally sensitive tourism programs as a strategy for sustainable development of urban ... settlements."[87]	This is a direct international lead-in to the concept of cultural tourism for (among other things) heritage districts.
Private Contracts	
The "law-making (which is) ad hoc and piecemeal" should be replaced by "a normative framework for economic planning and market instruments."[88]	This is perhaps the most crucial component of the entire sustainable development approach.

Recommendations (Abridged)	Commentary
Governments must adopt an "enabling" strategy, i.e., "incentives and facilitating measures for housing action to take place to a greater degree by other actors."[89]	The reference to this "enabling" strategy appears repeatedly in the *Global Strategy*; the fundamental premise is that governments must create a context in which other players can easily and efficiently ensure the achievement of the country's objectives. This notion of creating a positive climate for things to happen is identical to a recurring theme in the sustainable development texts, and the *Global Strategy* in fact refers specifically to sustainable shelter-delivery systems. The concept of "enabling other actors" has been interpreted in different ways; some countries are exploring whether rehabilitation skills could be supervised by a formal self-regulating association of contractors (on the guild model) and/or a warranty fund, i.e., an organization collecting a fee on all projects, to guarantee the skill of the work (this body would then have a huge interest in supervising craftsmanship, improving training, and expelling incompetent contractors).
Site-specific approaches "must give way to new concepts of establishing sustainable shelter-delivery systems that can operate at the required national scale."[90]	
Rehabilitation projects should observe modern safety standards, but when building codes and fire codes interfere with preservation, equivalents should be applied.[91]	In many countries, buildings undergoing major rehabilitation must meet the same standards as new construction. This creates a problem if (a) the legislation says that restored buildings must be exactly like new buildings (i.e., that the restoration cannot simply provide an equivalent level of safety, but must actually use the same materials and dimensions); or (b) the legislation specifies standards other than safety (like energy efficiency).

Recommendations (Abridged)	Commentary
Governments should establish technical consultative services[92], at the disposal of the private sector.[93]	"Information clearing houses" can guide owners towards intelligent cost-effective rehabilitation. However, in some countries, such a service would need to be protected against lawsuits.[94]
There should be a "program to develop national systems of an integrated environmental and economic accounting"[95] to create a generalized system of "new methods and rules of accounting for sustainable development."[96]	Many existing systems of accounting (e.g., systems of depreciation) were developed at a time when the world believed in "Planned Obsolescence," which is the exact opposite of sustainable development. Since systems of accounting are essential features of the overall economic system, this goal is as difficult as it is important.
There should be a policy of encouraging non-governmental organizations.[97]	In several countries, there are gigantic programs to protect heritage property without State intervention. For example, several Common Law countries use "easements" and "covenants" (called "servitudes" in Civil Law countries) so that private contracts can protect property (which remains in private ownership).
	Countries like the United States also favour the donation of property to non-government conservation organizations; in countries like the United Kingdom, this is a favoured way to reduce the likelihood of wealth taxes or inheritance taxes.

5. STATUTORY PRECEDENTS

5.1 The Original Model: Legislation for the Protection of Artistic Works

Origins in
Roman Law

The subject of legislation for the protection of significant heritage sites apparently begins in the year A.D. 457 with a statute passed under the reign of the Roman emperor Majorian.[98] That statute imposed the requirement of senatorial permits for any alteration or demolition at a variety of sites.

Revival in the
Renaissance

After the Dark Ages, the subject was resurrected by Pope Martin V who, in 1425, issued a ruling concerning construction that damaged ancient monuments. This was followed in 1462 by the Bull *Cum Alman Nostram Urbem* of Pope Pius II. Specific powers for the protection of ancient vestiges were delegated to the Antiquities Commission established by Pope Paul III in 1534. Protective legislation was enacted in nearby Tuscany in 1571.

The role of
inventories

In 1666, Sweden launched its famous inventory of historic sites, and this model eventually had significant influence throughout the legislation of the rest of Europe. Each important site was identified individually. At first, the Swedish inventory did not necessarily confer protection to that site; that legislation would come later. In other European governments, this approach evolved into the pattern of legislation today (starting with Würtemberg in 1790): legal protection would be conferred after the site had been placed on the inventory, and by necessary implication, the triggering mechanism for protection was a finding that the site met established criteria for that inventory.

Distinctive feature:
One-by-one
identification
and protection

In other words, the inventory would
- define the site (usually by precise geographic location),
- attest to its historical and/or architectural pedigree, and eventually (with each site being "evaluated according to its own merits"),
- confer protection, one site at a time.

Comparison
with museology

Since this species of legislation had its ultimate roots in a desire to protect great artistic works, it comes as no surprise that it evolved in parallel with museological legislation, for the protection of movable heritage. Over the course of years, this joint evolution of legislation has conferred a specific imprint to the statutory policies of the

"Monumental" pedigrees

countries that have adopted this model. Heritage buildings can supposedly be equated with artifacts: those are buildings whose educational/cultural dimensions have artifact quality. A "representative" sampling of buildings and districts of artifact quality may amount to 1 to 5 percent (seldom as much as 10 percent) of a country's total building stock. Words used to describe such artifacts include "monument," "*Denkmal,*" "landmark" or other words that signal how unusual that pedigree must be.[99]

Obligatory paper trails

That is the predominant working mandate that has been delivered to most governmental heritage programs. In day-to-day practice, this is exemplified by specific features:

Accessions

- detailed documentation must, by law or practice, accompany selections of property for the "heritage" label.
- The articulation of criteria becomes a crucial component of policy.
- Like a museum, the State must have an accessions policy to specify which sites get added to the list (and, sometimes, a "de-accessions policy" on which sites to drop). In some places, an entire industry has been launched for "heritage consultants" to advise on the heritage pedigree of sites to be added or deleted to the list.

Representativity

- The primary purpose of this kind of exercise is the collection of a representative sampling of buildings for illustrative cultural purposes. Although some redundancy is prudent (e.g., two or three examples of a given class of buildings), more widescale conservation (e.g., fifty to a hundred examples of a given class) is superfluity (except where a grouping constitutes a unit in its own right).

No tampering

- The overwhelming objective of legislative intervention is to prevent tampering. Artifacts are accepted in their as-is condition; even restoration should begin only after correct recording, to ensure no loss of cultural information on the artifact.

Identification by geography

Since each site is identified individually, a method must be used to identify the site legally. Typically, this will be done by a careful identification of its geographic location — accurate enough, for example, to allow any cartographer to draw lines on a map. The area inside the line is protected, whereas the area outside the line is not. In certain respects, this exercise is similar to the drawing of the boundaries of a park.

Vulnerability to attack for historicity

One crucial question in this category of legislation is whether a protective edict can be overturned in court, if someone (presumably the owner) challenges its credentials. For example, if a site has been listed for protection, can a court overrule that protection if the owner produces his/her own heritage consultants who testify that the site is of only mediocre national significance?

Objective test trap

This trap has occurred in the legislation in some jurisdictions where the statute has created an "objective test" specifying that only properties of historic or architectural importance can be listed and/or protected. For example, Australia has witnessed litigation over shipwrecks, where the court was called upon to decide between the claims of various expert witnesses in favour of or against the cultural significance of the find. As a result, courts find themselves ruling on cultural significance — an assignment that the court system was not expected to assume. An even more extreme case occurs when the legislation states that a building cannot be protected unless it is a certain number of years old.

Finality clauses

Other countries have blocked this possibility by declaring that the decision of public authorities on what is or is not heritage is final.

Eligibility for incentives

Once a country has introduced legislation for the protection of major artistic works, it is not unusual for it to add in that legislation that those works are eligible for certain economic incentives. Typically, those incentives will take the form of either cash measures or tax measures.

Statutory incentives

The cash incentives frequently come in the form of subsidies, low-interest loans or loan guarantees, all of which are usually specified in legislation. Tax incentives must be specified in legislation in order to exist, and these incentives can take a wide variety of forms, such as the French system of rapid tax-deductible depreciation or the American system of tax credits for approved restoration. Some countries like Belgium have adopted a wide variety of different measures simultaneously.

5.2 Statutes for the Protection of Buildings by *Genus*

Renaissance origins

A second category of legislation also draws its inspiration from the edicts of Majorian, Martin V and Paul III. Specific legislation, forbidding excavation without permits and requiring reporting of archaeological discoveries (within twenty-four hours), was produced by an edict of Cardinal Aldobrandini for the papal states in 1624.

Although the rationale for this legislation (as in the case of the previous category) was again cultural, the successors to this legislation definitely departed from the model initiated in Sweden in 1666 and Würtemberg in 1790.

Distinctive feature: Identification by class

Instead of relying upon a meticulously documented list of individually identified sites (each of which had been assessed according to pedigree), these statutes conferred blanket protection to any site (regardless of individual assessment) so long as the site fell within an identified generic category of properties.

Archaeological precedents

The tendency was seen in early archaeological legislation in a variety of countries; for example, they would provide automatic protection to all petroglyphs and prehistoric earthworks, so long as the site included these items. An actual evaluation of historic merit was not the pre-condition to the protection. It is this sort of approach that allowed Denmark, for example, to ultimately find itself with hundreds of thousands of protected archaeological sites within a relatively small national land mass.

National applications

Other countries extended this approach to different generic categories. Austria, for example, extended it to all sites with a religious use. Perhaps the most dramatic extension was done by Turkey,[100] which extended this form of protection to some fifty-two generic categories of properties, including everything from rock shelters and sarcophagi to mosque clock rooms and manufactories of silver thread.[101]

In this category of legislation, it is essential that the class be defined with sufficient clarity, so that both the public sector and the private sector can identify immediately whether a given property falls within that protected class.

Comparison: Endangered plants

By coincidence, this legislative model bears an uncanny resemblance to legislation for the protection of endangered species of plants or animals; the legislation is triggered as soon as it is acknowledged that the subject is a member of the species (it is not necessary to make an evaluation of the relative merits of the individual specimen).

In the twentieth century, one of the most wide-ranging categories of buildings to be protected is housing, which is mentioned again in the next section.

5.3 Land-use and Construction Legislation

In many countries, five main categories of legislation for local land use and development (usually under the jurisdiction of municipal governments) have a direct effect on the protection and/or restoration of buildings.

Controls on land use

a) Controls on land use *per se*. For example, if the planning legislation allowed a twenty-storey building on a site occupied by a two-storey building, that building would be threatened (unless there was no market demand for any building larger than the existing one).

Controls on normal construction quality

b) Controls on construction standards. The nature and severity of those standards, particularly when applied to alterations, can dramatically affect the kind and cost of restoration.

Protection of housing

c) Controls on the supply of housing. For example, some statutes (e.g., Ontario's) allow municipalities to prohibit the demolition of housing, unless the owner is legally obliged to replace that housing with the same (or greater) number of housing units than were there before. This is a kind of protective legislation that has relatively little to do with culture and nothing to do with the pedigree of a building.

Regulation of maintenance

d) Controls on the cleanliness and upkeep of property (again, this has nothing to do with pedigree).

"Historic districts"

e) "Historic districts." In certain countries such as the United States, protective legislation evolved as an offshoot of municipal land-use controls and particularly of the North American category of such controls called "zoning." Although the historical and/or architectural pedigree of the areas targeted for this treatment was relevant, the concept of harmony was at least as important. It is through the evolution of this category of legislation that Americans were first able to protect historic districts — which, paradoxically, became easier to protect (initially) than individual buildings.

Interplay of
legislation

In many countries, municipal and regional land-use controls continue to play a crucial role in the legislative future of old buildings. In some cases, it is because this category of legislation plays an essential complementary role: in Canada, for example, the issue of DBN ("Demolition By Neglect") is less of a problem than in the United States, because the obligation to maintain buildings does not face the same need to be specifically articulated in heritage legislation; it is a routine component of ordinary municipal property controls (called "property standards by-laws").

Potential
contradictions

Inversely, absurd situations can arise when plans to conserve or restore buildings have been overlooked by the rest of the municipal or regional land-use system. For example, some countries tax real estate according to an assessment of its development potential (for example, land will be taxed on the basis of the size of the development allowed by land-use controls). It is not unusual for owners in such countries to face the contradictory situation of having their land subjected to heritage controls (limiting them to the size of the existing building) while, simultaneously, being taxed as if the land could absorb a new real estate development five times larger.

5.4 "Environmental" Legislation

Buildings as
"environment"

Within the last thirty years, many governments have extended their environmental legislation to buildings. Although this legislation is sometimes affected by questions of historic or architectural pedigree, the ultimate driving force of these statutes is not culture (unlike many of the laws described earlier) but "environment" in the true sense. At any given time, the overwhelming majority of residents of urbanized countries are inside a building, and the majority of those buildings are in cities, towns and villages. It follows that at any given time, those buildings (and the accompanying community) constitute a more direct part of those residents' immediate "environment" than any other areas. In short, at most times of the day or night, urban civilization's immediate environment is a built environment. Buildings can be viewed as the human habitat, independently of pedigree.

Buildings and
waste control

Similarly, when environmentalists emphasized the principle of "re-use and recycle,"[102] one might expect some reference to the built environment, if only for purely pragmatic reasons. For example, approximately one-third of all landfill materials in a country like Canada is composed of "used construction material."[103] The re-use of buildings therefore becomes important for an entirely non-cultural reason, namely to avoid an impending garbage crisis.

Environmental impact assessments

This explains, in part, how some countries borrowed a procedure from their environmental legislation — namely, "environmental impact assessments" — and started extending it to buildings. Environmental impact assessments are a system popularized in countries such as Australia and the United States. Under this system, the State (and sometimes certain private companies) cannot alter or destroy a part of the landscape, unless a proper report has been filed to describe the expected results.

At first, that process tended to be confined to archaeological sites or to landmarks, but gradually spread to a progressively larger range of buildings.

Example of uses

For example, if the State is usually the largest single entrepreneur in a country (including capitalist countries), its own projects can have a significant impact on the built environment. The question is therefore whether the environmental impact assessment procedures will have an effect on government-funded projects that could have negative repercussions for that built environment. Although those procedures are clearly designed to screen effects on the natural environment, their role pertaining to the built environment is still in the development stages. In countries such as the United States[104] and Australia,[105] the central government is under a statutory obligation to protect at least heritage properties, if not the built environment generally.[106]

Specific example

The U.S.[107] National Historic Preservation Act (1966) is a noteworthy example of how the scope of this kind of legislation can expand.

- Originally, it targeted only properties that were on the U.S. National Register of important landmarks; impact assessments were required when those registered properties were threatened by any initiative that was federally funded.

Progressive expansion

- By the same token, injunctions could be applied for (e.g., by citizens' groups) when a National Register property was threatened but the assessment procedure had been circumvented or overlooked.

- In 1976, the U.S. legislation was expanded to include properties that were not on a national register, but on a supplementary list of properties "eligible" for the National Register.[108]
- Between 1981 and 1985, a web of further regulations was systematically introduced, creating a new cumulative effect; it was now a positive legal duty on the part of federal officials to inventory all sites that met a specified list of *Criteria for Eligibility*, published in another regulation. The effect in the jurisprudence was straightforward: when a community group had evidence that a totally unlisted property objectively met those criteria, it could apply for an injunction compelling its inclusion in the list of "eligible" property and (collaterally) blocking any destruction until the consequential assessment procedures (which flow from inclusion on the list) had been complied with.

Outdoing "natural" environment legislation

The effect of s. 106 today is therefore to create a screening procedure that can be invoked for all properties which intrinsically meet the historical and/or architectural standards laid out in the *Criteria for Eligibility*. It is now the view of the senior counsel of the U.S. Advisory Council on Historic Preservation that the s. 106 procedure functions more methodically and predictably than the U.S. environmental impact procedures for the natural environment.[109]

5.5 The Shift Towards Sustainable Development

Moving away from geographically based planning

More sweeping legal measures to address "the built environment as a whole," were occasionally discussed in various countries, but these did not acquire momentum until the 1987 report on sustainable development, which electrified world public opinion. The embryonic statutory response is described next.

Much of the world's population is urbanized; consequently, when the Brundtland Commission[110] called for sustainable development, one might have expected at least some attention to be devoted to sustainable urban development.

Sustainable development implies a different kind of planning compared to what most countries have been used to. Traditionally, planning included the drawing of lines on maps to demarcate respective areas of "conservation" and "development." This process often resulted in an adversarial relationship between the public and private sectors over which side of the line their property was on. With the advent of the principle of sustainable development, this approach to demarcation has been blurred. This is partly because of intrinsic characteristics of the concept — and partly because, as a new concept, it still means different things to different people.

Distinctive feature

The abiding feature of this approach, however, is that it invites populations to reflect on their development patterns systemically:

- The question is not how do we introduce a veto on a negative feature of development; but
- the question instead is whether society can identify and remedy the causes of such negative features before they even start.

Buildings as economic resources

For example, why are our cities and landscapes the way they are? For every result, there is a cause, so the question is this: what are the causal factors that drive our development patterns to be or not be sustainable?

Furthermore, this category of investments represents perhaps the largest inventory of assets on which many countries have no policy whatever pertaining to use or re-use. This oversight exists despite the fact that this environment has a substantial mass, volume and visibility:

- It is estimated that in most industrialized countries, there is at least one building (residential, commercial, industrial, religious, agricultural) for every three inhabitants;
- the capital investment represented by this collection (regardless of pedigree) is staggering;
- normally, one would expect that with an inventory of that economic magnitude, every country would have a public policy on whether to upgrade it, replace it, or do something else with it; one would not expect that kind of inventory to be merely ignored, any more than one would expect a country to disregard how it would deal with other major inventories such as its oil reserves, fish stocks, forestry reserves or other collections of assets.

If both officials and the public could become concerned about the re-use and recycling of items as small as pop bottles and tin cans, one would expect interest in the re-use or recycling of items as large as entire buildings, neighbourhoods and cities.

Specific
example: Tax

One immense example is frequently cited. In an economically driven system of urban development, the tax system can be a larger "form-giver" to cities than all architects and planners put together.

Tax rules: A
product of
their era
(1940s)

The tax system is not neutral. It has distinctive features that it has conferred on urban development patterns, which is not surprising when one remembers that the income tax system of many countries was designed in the 1930s or 1940s, at precisely the time when conventional wisdom was dominated by the desire to replace entire cities. This perspective[111] coloured the new tax system in many countries; old buildings were disfavoured, demolition was encouraged and "planned obsolescence" was promoted in exactly the era when accounting principles were being developed to harmonize with the new tax laws. Where the income tax statute was silent, the blanks would be filled in by "Generally Accepted Accounting Principles" (GAAP). It was accepted wisdom that

- in countries such as the United States and Canada, the overwhelming majority of buildings (which are built of wood-frame construction) would lose some two-thirds of their real value within a decade of their purchase;
- masonry and steel-framed buildings would lose a third of their real value;
- demolition was good and would result in a significant tax deduction for the owner when it occurred (in Canada for example, demolition received even better tax treatment than a donation of the building to charity);
- re-use, renovation and repair would not be significant factors (the words "repair" and "renovation," although fiscally crucial,[112] did not even warrant definition).

Urban
consequences

This view of GAAP was so entrenched among bureaucrats and accountants that countless owners of rental buildings found themselves overdepreciating their property and were faced with the prospect of tax penalties when they sold. The way to avoid those penalties was to demolish — and demolition entitled them to further deductions. In real estate investments, profit margins are often narrow enough that even a slight fiscal distortion is enough to tip the balance between re-use and replacement of older buildings. After forty years, the results were predictable: in countries with such systems, downtowns were indeed largely levelled — as predicted with the help of the taxpayers. Other countries that refused to take this fiscal approach found themselves with dramatically different patterns of urban development.

This situation suggests five conclusions:

1. In many countries with similar accounting and tax systems, the principle of "sustainability" was not historically — and is not now — a feature of the economic system's approach to urban development.
2. Tax officials are the "silent partners" of all private sector decision makers; as such they are "form-givers" in the urban context to a greater extent than almost all planners.
3. People have the cities they paid for (and that they are still paying for).
4. If one wishes to bring sustainable development (and the concepts of re-use and recover) to civilization's largest products, namely cities, one should have no illusions about the work ahead.
5. It is arguably insufficient to propose a "tax incentive" for buildings — when the purpose of that incentive is to counterbalance a disincentive that threatens buildings generally. The more logical objective would be to eliminate the disincentive in the first place.

Goal: For good development "to take care of itself"

The ultimate goal of the sustainable development movement is no less than (1) to encourage an economic climate in which people pursue this development not because they are guided by the State, but because it is the economically reasonable thing to do and (2) to ensure that such a scenario gets fair and even-handed treatment (legally and fiscally).

If countries can move towards that goal, they can reduce the adversarial relationship between the public and private sectors and foster a planning system where partnership takes precedence over drawing lines on maps.

Pedigree irrelevant

This view, however, is at the opposite end of the spectrum from the one underlying legislation for artistic works, because legislation for sustainable development has little to do with culture and nothing to do with pedigree. It views buildings as working components of the "built environment," which should be subjected to the same principles of "sustainable development" that the Brundtland Commission recommended for the environment as a whole.

By that reasoning, national strategy is led to certain positions that are the diametric opposite of the policies described earlier for buildings of "artifact" value. Some of those contrasts are the following:

The opposite of "artifacts"

- National policies of sustainable development need to be developed for 100 percent of the existing building stock, not just the 1 to 10 percent of artifact value.
- Sustainable development theory starts from the premise that buildings should be viewed first as "investments" whose economic lifespan should be extended, even if only for that reason. The notion of creating these investments, then replacing them at every third generation, would be rejected on the ground that it is non-sustainable.
- There is no need to establish a pedigree (cultural or otherwise) for buildings to enjoy the benefits of sustainable development (e.g., extension of "life expectancy" and periodic upgrading).
- Superfluity among buildings targeted for "an extension of economic life expectancy" is irrelevant.
- The overwhelming objective of legislative (and other) intervention, in the case of these investments is the same as for all investments. It is "to optimize the investment." "Ask not what you shouldn't do with the property, but what you should do with it."

Sweeping objectives

The rehabilitation of the entire existing building stock is, in many respects, an environmentalist's ideal sustainable industry. Not only does it extend the economic lifespan of existing investments, but it is a large employer that allows cities to enhance their own economic value (in many countries, residential renovation spending exceeds new construction) without a corresponding draw on natural resources, and without putting extra pressure on the urban infrastructure, including sewers, roads, refuse disposal, etc.

This perspective, however, is not unanimous, and the kinds of controversies that result for national legislative strategy are described next.

6. PROTECTIVE LEGISLATION — AT A CROSSROADS

6.1 Some Difficult Choices

Background to the debate
The UNESCO recommendations refer to national, regional and local strategies for the protection of property (at least in the case of heritage buildings), but that is not as easy an assignment as it may sound. For example, there are still many countries that assume that as long as they have introduced a governmental veto on the private destruction of "universal" monuments (such as those on

For "heritage"
UNESCO's World Heritage List), then they have fulfilled their treaty obligation to "integrate heritage into the life of the community," and their legislation needs to proceed no further.

For other buildings
Others disagree; some observers argue that historical and/or architectural pedigree is not even at the centre of the issue of protective legislation at all (an argument that, not surprisingly, horrifies some architectural historians).

Some examples of how this debate can affect national legislative strategies are described below. The most dramatic contrasts between legislative strategies occur between

- theories that are based on the classic "artifact" approach to landmark legislation, as compared to
- theories based on the objective of "sustainable development" in the "built environment."

6.2 Site-Specific Solutions

Ad hoc characteristics
Most countries, particularly those with artifact-type legislation, have a fundamentally site-specific approach to the protection of buildings. This approach has distinct characteristics:

- Despite attempts to put identification and listing of heritage sites onto a footing to provide substantial lead time before critical decisions must be made on the property, many situations must still be dealt with on an *ad hoc* basis.

- That is not perceived as fatal, however, because the site is reputedly dealt with on its own merits.
- By the same token, the solutions for the site also tend to be dealt with "on their own merits," with *ad hoc* remedies tailored to that specific site. For example, if it is discovered that legislation of general application impedes the conservation or restoration of the site, an exemption would be sought to waive the application of the legislation to this site. (The heritage agency may even attempt to secure an exemption for all designated sites.)

Ad hoc economic arrangements

Similarly, if various economic forces appear to be militating against the property, these may reputedly be compensated by a special grant or subsidy for the site (and possibly even a series of unusual tax incentives applicable to an entire sub-class of designated heritage properties).

6.3 Looking Beyond the Site-Specific: The Systemic Approach

The above governmental methodology has been accused (particularly by sustainable development advocates) of suffering from four closely related but fundamental liabilities:

A different definition of objectives

1. If legislation threatens older buildings, the long-term solution is allegedly not just to secure an exemption on élite properties: it is to amend the legislation. "The objective is not just to react to the symptom, but cure the disease."
2. If economic forces threaten older buildings, the long-term solution is not to "compensate" for them in isolated cases; it is to redirect those economic forces (same rationale as above).

The hospital analogy

3. Governmental intervention on a site-specific basis is arguably only a last resort when there has been a failure of the general real estate system of the country to adequately protect its important building stock. This intervention is, for buildings, what hospitals are for people: an emergency response to sick cases. The equipment for that intervention should be as advanced as possible, but the higher priority remains preventive

medicine, i.e., creating a healthy context for the population (or building stock) as a whole.

4. As long as legal or economic factors are stacked against older buildings, heritage authorities will always be in a reactive position in their attempt to cope with crises, rather than a proactive position to control the agenda. If one wishes to move beyond "crisis management," the only recourse is to redirect overall legal and economic forces to a posture more favourable to the re-use of older buildings.

The debate on whether "to focus or not to focus"

According to sustainable development theorists, this interest in whether "the deck was stacked" against older buildings generally compels consideration of the fate of the entirety of "the built environment," i.e., 100 percent of the existing building stock. That line of reasoning, however, drew four distinct points of criticism from some observers, particularly those who preferred to retain the emphasis on historical and/or architectural pedigree:

Accusations over pedigree

• the protective agency's mandate usually did not extend to factors affecting the rest of the building stock, but only those that immediately affected the 1 to 5 percent of the building stock that was on their list as being designated (or "designatable") as "national heritage";

Retrenchment

• there was nothing among the generalized legal or economic forces affecting the entirety of the building stock that would necessarily be fatal to them: these legal or economic forces could be compensated (in relation to the 1 to 2 percent of the designated "heritage" building stock), through *ad hoc* exemptions, waivers and subsidies;

• exploration of the issues affecting the larger building stock (up to 100 percent) would not only carry heritage officials out of their realm of expertise, but would expose them to ridicule from other government agencies;

• in any event, heritage agencies lacked the resources (nor should they have any fundamental interest) to pursue issues that affected buildings with no heritage characteristics.

Where is housing sector

This debate, of course, ignored the housing sector altogether, as if it did not even exist. The housing industry and housing officials have their own agenda, which appears to have been overlooked by the other groups. However, that is only one of several anomalies, as described below.

6.4 Strategic Consequences

An uneasy partnership

The above controversy created a dilemma. In some countries (e.g., in North America) the advocates of "artifact buildings" and of the "built environment" (though seldom of "housing") all purportedly gathered under the same banner of "the heritage movement"; but at the core of their respective objectives lay fundamentally different philosophies that caused awkward situations for a heritage agency caught between the confines of its own administrative mandate and the urgency of "curing diseases instead of reacting to symptoms."

Tactical example: Which "growth potential" do we cite?

For example, a heritage agency could feel torn in how it framed its argument for stronger interdepartmental support for its efforts.

- The advocates of "artifact buildings" within the agency often believed that the growth of "cultural tourism" showed that there was still a huge untapped level of public support for their educational and cultural publicity that could translate into growing support for heritage artifacts (hence promising political benefits for larger heritage budgets).
- Advocates of the "built environment" sometimes disagreed. They argued that in many locations, surveys indicated roughly the same percentage of public support as there was twenty years ago. That led some of them to a critical strategic decision: "If we are going to grow at all, it will only be if we play the environmental card."
- People interested in housing, in the meantime, appeared to be separate from this discussion altogether.

6.5 Three Philosophies

A hybrid view

Some organizations[113] attempted to fuse these views into a hybrid position, incorporating the following points:

- The entirety of the existing building stock is a "built environment" to which rules of sustainable development must be applied on a systemic basis.

- A part of that *continuum*, in addition, constitutes either "housing" or "heritage" that should enjoy special treatment.
- However, society must be capable of addressing all of these dimensions.
- In order to do so, society would have to equip itself with a broad range of legal tools and approaches, which would vary depending on whether the target was an individual item (at one extreme) or an entire national landscape (at the other extreme).

In summary, three distinct views emerged.

- The "artifact" view: society must identify and protect its buildings of educational and cultural value; this view is reflected in most legislative apparatus.
- The "sustainable environmental" view: society must entrench rules of sustainable development for the entirety of its building stock in order to extend its "investment" value (quite independently of educational and cultural considerations); this view is based on the international documents and would get a sympathetic ear among associations representing the repair and restoration industry.
- A "hybrid view": society must develop rules for the entirety of its built environment, as well as certain special adjustments for its properties of social, educational and cultural value.

Disagreements   This division of opinion elicited some behind-the-scenes acrimony at certain conferences.

- The advocates of the "artifact" philosophy sometimes treated advocates of the "built environment" as slumming, or at least of diluting the subject matter of heritage beyond recognition.
- The latter accused the former (and their site-specific focus on the top strata of buildings) of taking such a narrow view as to marginalize the protection and rehabilitation of buildings right off the political agenda, ignoring systemic issues and confining themselves to *ad hoc* interventions. Furthermore, they argued that even in countries where 10 percent of the building stock was protected, that still left 90 percent exposed and doomed heritage advocates to a perennially reactive posture.

Many conferences also addressed whether a proper balance had been struck between

- the "limits on a property-owners' freedoms" and
- "the increase in their costs."

This thorny issue underlines, in perhaps the most dramatic terms, the ongoing difference in perspective between the "artifact" view and the "investment" view. If one starts from the premise that a building is an artifact, then

Negative vs. positive instructions

(a) there is a duty to tamper with its "as-is" condition as little as possible;

(b) all existing features (including, perhaps, even its deterioration) are testimonies to its history, and any tampering must be viewed with great circumspection, for fear of altering the authenticity of the cultural experience;

"Protective authenticity"

(c) of necessity, the thrust of legislative intervention will be negative — it will focus on restraining those who hold the property from tampering with it inappropriately.

"Promoting investment" or "re-use"

If the property is viewed primarily as an "investment," the reverse is true: the objective, with investments, is for them to be "optimized."

(a) It would follow that governmental intervention, at least as popularly perceived, would not be negative (i.e., restraining something), but rather positive (i.e., promoting something).

(b) In this case, the objective would be to draw maximum "benefit" (however defined) from the "resource" in question.

(c) In a real estate context, that would translate into directives that are less focused on regulation than on instruction as to what best to do (positively) with the property.

Psychological impact

That is not the orientation of many governmental programs or planning systems. Sustainable development theorists have argued that this has represented a gigantic liability for efforts to protect buildings, for two reasons:

- Property owners resent instructions on what not to do with their property, more than suggestions on what to do (which, indeed, are often welcomed).
- Furthermore, any marketing expert will agree that it is immeasurably more difficult to "sell" an idea that is phrased in the negative than one that is phrased in the positive.

It is therefore argued that governmental strategy,

which is formulated exclusively in the negative, imposes a political liability upon itself.

The ultimate outcome of this debate is expected to affect the perceived role of public administration. That result is described next.

7. DE FACTO PROTECTION VERSUS DE JURE PROTECTION

7.1 Relevance and Status Quo

A "positive climate" for buildings

Although much of the discussion of protective legislation focuses on statutes that confer formal legal protection (*de jure* protection), this is not the only area of legislative intervention in the fate of buildings; some would argue that it is not even the principal area.

According to this reasoning (favoured, in particular, by the "sustainable development" advocates), the higher priority is to use subtle legislative strategy to create a pervasive system that leads owners "naturally" towards the protection and rehabilitation of their buildings, without visible State intervention. If owners are induced to lean in that direction, then the building will enjoy protection in real life ("*de facto*").

"Uncompetitiveness"

Most buildings (not only in western countries) enjoy *de facto* protection through the free market: they are already competitive (with replacement structures or uses) in their existing condition. Many would, of course, be even more competitive if properly renovated or restored.

On the other hand, in most countries, the number of buildings enjoying *de jure* protection varies widely. The major variable is the level of legal protection attached to housing. If the planning legislation bans destruction of housing, then 30 to 40 percent of the total building stock may have *de jure* protection, but otherwise the figure drops dramatically. In most countries less than 5 percent of the building stock enjoys *de jure* protection under any of the heritage statutes in the country; this applies to both buildings and districts. Many of those that are so protected (because they are either "housing" or "heritage") were chosen precisely because there were fears

- that the rehabilitation of the buildings was intrinsically uncompetitive from an economic standpoint, and
- that direct governmental intervention was therefore essential to conserve and/or upgrade the buildings.

Limitations to scope

Any focus on *de facto* protection through competitiveness excludes many sites where the topic is inappropriate, such as churches, palaces and archaeological sites, but even public buildings such as government headquarters and courthouses must "compete" in their own way with offers of newer space.

In the private sector, where the overwhelming majority of older buildings are located (in most non-communist countries), competitiveness is the lifeblood of survival.

7.2 The Regulation/Subsidy Trap

How "uncompetitiveness" affected public administration

The assumption that older buildings are uncompetitive led many governments into the logical trap of assuming that

- the regulatory mechanism was the appropriate way for governments to intervene on a site-specific basis.
- Alternatively, governments could launch subsidy programs to artificially compensate for "intrinsic uncompetitiveness," again on a site-specific basis.
- Relatively less attention was addressed to solving the competitive problem by making the protection/rehabilitation option more competitive, either on a site-specific or generalized basis.

Policy questions

Advocates of the "built environment" argue that this overlooking of competitiveness was predictable, particularly on the part of the fans of "artifact buildings."

- Among artifacts, competitiveness is not an issue. The government role, in relation to artifacts, is usually to regulate the items and/or to subsidize them by grants, loans or other means.
- Among "investments," however, the role of government is usually perceived differently. If the item is uncompetitive, one of the first questions is typically whether the government itself is partly to blame for its uncompetitiveness.

Action and reaction

This opens up a vast area of enquiry, namely the scope of governmental policies that (advertently or inadvertently) artificially undermine the competitiveness of older buildings, render them unable to enjoy *de facto* protection, and hence force them into a crisis position.

7.3 The Definition of "Repair" and "Restoration"

The calculation
of taxable
"profit"

In many countries, the so-called "economic realities" are heavily affected by artificial government systems that militate against the free market competitiveness of the older building stock. Some of these have been buried deep in the country's accounting system. For example, most countries have an income tax system that taxes the profit from the occupancy of real estate (rental residential, commercial, industrial, agricultural).

Repairs vs. additions

Impact

The rules that define how to calculate profit can be crucial: in most systems, "repairs" are considered to reduce taxable profit, but "additions" are not. Is restoration a "repair" or an "addition"? If it is a repair, its cost would be deductible from taxable profit — which is usually far more attractive than when the cost must be entirely borne by the owner (i.e., without any significant tax deductions). This issue can have such a dramatic effect on the profitability of restoration (and the profitability of the building itself) that it is often the largest single legal issue to affect the *de facto* fate of older buildings.

Confrontation
with tax
officials

In a country like Canada, the courts have issued definitions of the word "repair" that encompass most restoration projects. Tax officials, however, have so far refused to comply. The dispute over these definitions (which were decided for legal reasons, not because of any sympathy for heritage) is perhaps the largest single artificial disincentive of the Canadian government *vis-à-vis* restoration activity. Other countries would have a similar interest in re-examining their own counterparts.

7.4 Technological Appropriateness of Construction Standards

In many countries, a person who proposes to undertake a major rehabilitation project must demonstrate that the finished building will meet the construction standards or codes established by the State.

State
demands on
rehabilitation
projects

Many worthwhile renovations and restorations are frustrated by inappropriate building standards or codes that were designed for new buildings but that fail to recognize renovation techniques that could render restored buildings as safe as new construction, albeit by different means (these different means are sometimes called "equivalents").

Similarly, rehabilitation may become artificially uneconomical, if the State demands that, for reasons having nothing to do with safety, the restored building must perform differently than it did before — for example, that it must have a much higher level of energy efficiency.

Flexibility in
standards

The effect of these awkward code provisions on proposed restorations can be economically disastrous, which then affects cost-benefit and often the fate of the building. Various groups have demanded a more sophisticated codification of renovation practice to facilitate the legal use of these technologies.

7.5 Education Programs and Guarantees of Competence

The effect of
training on
competitive-
ness

The cost-efficiency of the conservation, renovation or restoration of heritage property can fluctuate depending on the knowledge, skills and planning process of the team responsible for the work. The choice of the wrong technology can not only increase costs, but threaten the building. In the short term, training and information programs are crucial for all professionals, entrepreneurs, trades and workers.

Disproportion-
ate risk

In some countries, a system is in place to ensure the availability of trained personnel for restoration projects on the tiny minority of government-listed heritage buildings but on nothing else. Any ordinary citizen who wishes to ensure the *de facto* conservation of his/her building is left with a high level of risk in the selection of competent personnel for the project. This risk is compounded when there is no reliable system of warranties for work conducted. The risk not only constitutes a deterrent, but also fosters a breeding ground for black market renovations — often resulting in disproportionately low quality for the money spent.

There are three main avenues (or a combination thereof) for a response to this problem:

Information clearing houses	a) **Information clearing houses:** These are services (provided by governments, NGOs and/or industry) to inform owners about reputable professionals, contractors and trades who are knowledgeable about particular kinds of rehabilitation.
Certification/ licensing	b) **Certification or licensing of competent contractors/trades:** This is comparable to the German *Meister* system. Often, the licensing is done by the State, but in some areas, it is proposed that the licensing be done by the repair/restoration industry itself (the industry would operate its own licensing program via its own members, in the same manner as lawyers' societies, colleges of physicians and other professions).
Warranties	c) **A building rehabilitation warranty system:** Depending on how the system is designed, it could become the most dramatic legal tool in shifting the supervision of quality control on rehabilitation projects out of the hands of the State, into the hands of a non-governmental organization.

7.6 Government Occupancy of Older Buildings

Discrimination

As difficult as it is for private sector heritage buildings to obtain tenants (and hence improve economic prospects), the situation is usually worse in the public sector. Many industrial countries (and some notable Third World countries) are littered with instances of governments

- refusing to use space in their own heritage buildings, and
- refusing to lease rehabilitated buildings because these were not what "prestigious governmental space was supposed to look like."

Possible statutes

This phenomenon, sometimes called the "Brasilia Syndrome," can occasionally reach absurd extremes. The U.S. Congress was so irritated at a similar situation in Washington that Congress legislated its own bureaucrats into using their own heritage space[114] — but even that legislation failed. This is an issue of "bureaucratic culture" that not only restricts by artificial means the market for heritage property, but also discredits the government's own heritage agency; for how can a government agency persuade the private sector of the virtue of re-using heritage buildings if its own colleagues refuse to do so? This is a problem that does not appear to have an easy statutory solution and one that requires further attention.

7.7 Income Tax Give-aways for Demolition

The disappearance of buildings

In many countries, the tax rules affect how the country's accounting system will deal with a building that has been demolished. If the building was held for investment purposes, how should its disappearance be entered in the taxpayers' ledger?

Tax consequences of disappearance

In some countries (e.g., Canada and the United States), the fact that the building was there one day and is absent the next is, on the instruction of the tax statute, entered as a "loss," and all or part of the supposed value of the building (at the time of this "loss"), is entered in the ledger as having been similarly "lost." Some countries (e.g., Canada and the United States) then provide that since the investor has now suffered an investment loss, this destruction will result in all or part of the asset's value (as listed in the ledger immediately prior to demolition) being deducted from taxable income.

In countries where the tax laws adopt this approach, it can represent a massive national tax giveaway encouraging the demolition of buildings.

7.8 Other Tax Give-aways for Demolition, Notably Property Taxes

Property/ wealth taxes on rehabilitation or demolition

Independently of taxes on income, many countries have a tax applicable to the value of property — i.e., its market value (or a proportion thereof), its "deemed rental" value, its role in accumulated "wealth," etc. The question is whether this system, in a given jurisdiction,

• penalizes individuals who restore property and/or
• rewards those who convert it to vacant land.

For example, parking lots enjoy among the most preferential kinds of business tax treatment under the typical provincial assessment legislation in Canada (Ontario's Assessment Act imposed a business tax on retail buildings several times the amount charged for a parking lot assessed at *identical* value). On the other hand, renovation or restoration often increases property taxes, which is not perceived as much of an incentive for "doing the right thing" with one's property.

7.9 Tax Systems that Insist on Short Life Expectancies for Buildings

Depreciation

In some tax systems (e.g., the United Kingdom), there is no system of depreciation that would allow the building's accountants to devalue the building annually on the proprietor's ledger.

In the absence of "depreciation", if an investment property was worth £100,000 on the owner's ledger in 1980, it would still be listed at £100,000 on the ledger in 1990. [In real life, that accounting system can indeed acknowledge that the building lost value — for whatever reason — since £100,000 in 1990 had less value (because of inflation) than £100,000 had in 1980. That tax system is saying, in effect, that the erosion in market value is no greater than the erosion in the value of money, and hence the two figures remain equal to each other.]

Cataclysmic (and tax-deductible) declines in value

In other tax systems (e.g., Canada and the United States), the tax system provides an automatic right to claim that the building has been devalued beyond a figure corresponding to inflation. For example, under Canada's current treatment of an investment building that was entered in the owner's ledger in 1984 at a value of $100,000, it would be listed, by 1994, as having a remaining value of approximately $66,000; the other $34,000 would be treated as the depreciation or devaluation of the building, and would be tax-deductible. In other words, the building was treated as having lost one-third of its value before adjusting for inflation; after adjusting for inflation and the decline in the value of money, the building would be treated as having lost (in "constant dollars") over half (53 percent) of its value.

Resulting fiscal trap

In real life, buildings in Canada seldom lost value (beyond inflation), and this created a problem. Owners who routinely reduce their taxes every year by deducting depreciation face a dilemma: as soon as they sell their buildings at more than their depreciated figure on their ledgers, the unreality of their "depreciation" is exposed, and the system provides that tax authorities can reclaim tax retroactively on all the unjustified depreciation that comes to light. One way to avoid this tax liability is by demolishing the building prior to sale.

This tax avoidance at demolition, combined with the tax treatment of "losses" incurred at demolition (described earlier), can become a powerful though artificial rationale for the destruction of buildings for redevelopment, instead of their re-use. Any country that has a comparable system for tax-deductible depreciation of buildings may similarly be planting fiscal time-bombs in its building stock.

7.10 Discriminatory Subsidies to Public Buildings

Higher subsidies for replacement

There are numerous examples of government subsidy programs for schools, hospitals, universities and other public institutions that vigorously discriminate against repair and rehabilitation in favour of demolition and replacement — for example, by providing disproportionately higher subsidies for replacement than repair. This clearly distorts the economics of older public buildings and threatens their legitimate life expectancy.

7.11 Artificial Restrictions on Financing

Bank discrimination against heritage

Some countries have an overwhelmingly private sector banking system; others have a nationalized state bank, purportedly to assist national objectives. Some countries have a combination of both. At least one state bank is known to have advised applicants that it is unlikely to finance projects secured by mortgages on listed heritage property, because it considers such collateral security as essentially worthless. The reason, says the bank, is that it does not like the "red tape" involved once those properties have been listed. This is clearly a serious obstacle to any such restoration project.

7.12 Disregarding Philanthropic Expenditures

Tax deductibility

The income tax system of most countries acknowledges that business expenses are totally tax-deductible. In many countries, however, philanthropic or charitable expenditures are treated much worse than business expenses; a donor cannot claim the whole expense as a tax deduction if he/she donated it for the public good.

Fiscal discrimination

In countries like Canada, the charitable deduction is eroded by fiscal fictions; in the United Kingdom, the deduction is non-existent. In short, a taxpayer receives more favourable treatment when squandering an asset for (mistakenly) avaricious motives than when giving it away for idealistic motives. This imbalance is a deterrent to any taxpayer who wants to save property by donating it to conservation agencies or by reaching some other arrangement that voluntarily relinquishes part of his/her property rights.

8. New Economic Parameters

> "In many cases, public authorities have failed to understand the effects of laws and regulations on incentives and costs, with the result that they have increased the cost of housing, lowered the productivity of the sector, skewed inequitably the benefits of the housing sector and had a damaging effect on overall economic performance."
>
> *Global Strategy for Shelter*[115]

8.1 "The Market" and the Role of Government Agencies

The priority of "fairness"

On one hand, there will always be a minority of buildings that are outside the operation of commercial market forces (churches, for example). On the other hand, it is argued that a much larger segment of the threatened older building stock may not need "incentives," "perks," "subsidies," etc. to be competitive. The older building stock simply needs a level playing field. If it were to obtain that level playing field, a much larger percentage of the building stock would enjoy *de facto* protection, and the cumbersome process of applying *de jure* protection would not even be necessary, except in a minority of cases.

Scepticism over grants and tax incentives

This can be compared with the argument that a more generous system of government grants or tax incentives should be made available for the repair or re-use of heritage buildings. That argument has been criticized for three reasons:

What "the government gives, the government takes away..."

• All subsidy systems are already under attack for budgetary reasons, particularly in view of today's world economy.

• The typical subsidy systems, whether for housing or heritage, exclude the overwhelming majority of older buildings, including many worthy of repair (at least in the minds of some).

- Perhaps most controversially, so-called "artificial" economic instruments, such as subsidies and tax incentives, are almost always the most vulnerable to cutback during a recession: to rely on them is to invite an artificial boom-and-bust cycle in the rehabilitation or repair industry.

This last point is perhaps the largest single reason why the focus, in some countries, has shifted to methods to encourage the competitiveness of older buildings, via long-term systemic adjustments that could be synthesized with the overall economic system, without any taint of artificiality.

The first step, described below in more detail, was clearly to identify and eliminate the existing governmental disincentives affecting the built environment.

8.2 National Strategies

Renovation strategy

In some countries, the process of re-establishing a fair economic treatment of older buildings begins by reconsidering the building repair, renovation and restoration industry as a whole, and undertaking a strategy for its health in the twenty-first century.

For example, the Canadian residential renovation industry is developing a detailed gameplan to develop a better context for work on older buildings. Although the execution of that gameplan is still in its earliest stages, it encompasses a list of specific goals, including

- the development of a multi-decade strategic plan for personnel training to improve cost efficiency,
- feasibility studies for comprehensive warranty programs on workmanship,
- the clarification and updating of the tax treatment of rehabilitation,
- the systemization of intelligent "alternative measures" for safe rehabilitation of buildings (as opposed to the current construction codes that often prove extremely awkward and potentially counterproductive on renovation projects), and
- the curtailment of the black market in renovations (which often prove shoddy).

Policies of
"resource
protection

This approach is based on one fundamental assumption. Unlike most other resources, buildings cannot be protected by merely leaving them alone. Unless there is a conscious strategy to maintain them (and occasionally upgrade their systems), they either fall down or are swept away by competing uses for the same land.

Components of
National
Strategy

By that reasoning, it is impossible to develop a proper national legislative strategy for the protection of buildings unless it is accompanied by a legislative strategy for their rehabilitation, and a comprehensive analysis of all legislation that may explain why the building would be threatened in the first place.

9. HABITAT II: RECONCILIATION OF POSITIONS

9.1 Salutory Effects

U.N.
Conference

In the early 1990s, the heritage community was feeling the effects of economic and budgetary changes in many countries. This added to the malaise which was evident at some expert meetings, over whether heritage could best be approached incrementally (by addressing meritorious "cultural properties" one by one, as had been done in the past) or collectively (by immediately addressing the built environment as a whole). The positions advanced by advocates of the "artifact" philosophy and of "sustainable development" might have continued to cause tension within the international heritage community for years to come, were it not for the intervention of the Second United Nations Conference on Human Settlements ("Habitat II"). This major conference, on a par with the Rio de Janeiro Earth Summit which adopted *Agenda 21*, was held in Istanbul in 1996. In essence, it endorsed both views, with the obvious inference that a Member-State could and should approach the subject of buildings from both directions simultaneously.

Two-pronged
declaration

The international community, as represented by the governments which participated in the final declarations (including almost every national government on earth) vindicated the so-called "hybrid" policy which recognizes the importance of both

- an elite body of monuments, historic groupings and other examples of architectural heritage, as well as

- a systemic approach to the rehabilitation of the building stock as a whole.

The Habitat
Agenda

The conference's recommendations to U.N. Member-States are published in a document entitled *The Habitat Agenda*. This document encapsulates much of the previous strategic thinking that had been implicit in the UNESCO Recommendations, the *Global Strategy for Shelter* and *Agenda 21* — but which had not been specifically integrated and applied to architecture and the built environment generally. In that respect, *The Habitat Agenda* can be treated as a watershed in the evolution of the international community's strategic approach in this topic.

9.2 Proposed Initiatives

Assertions of the
Assembled
States

The role of heritage buildings is outlined both early and frequently in this lengthy document. The following extracts convey a flavour of the forceful language used:

- "We, the States participating in the United Nations Conference on Human Settlements (Habitat II) further commit ourselves to the objectives of...protecting and maintaining the historic, cultural and natural heritage....[116]
- The quality of life of all people depends, among other economic, social, environmental and cultural factors, on the physical conditions and spatial characteristics of our villages, towns and cities. City layout and aesthetics ... and public amenities have a crucial bearing on the livability of settlements... Peoples' need for community and their aspirations for more liveable neighbourhoods and settlements should guide the process of design, management and maintenance of human settlements. Objectives of this endeavour include ... preservation of historic, spiritual, religious and culturally significant buildings and districts, respecting local landscapes and treating local environment with respect and care. The preservation of natural heritage and historical human settlements including sites, monuments and buildings ... should be assisted, including through international cooperation.[117]
- Governments should...integrate land and shelter policies with policies ... for creating jobs, for environmental protection, for preservation of the cultural heritage, for education and health....[118]
- Historical places, objects...and manifestations of cul-

tural and scientific, symbolic, spiritual and religious values are important expressions of the culture, identity and religious beliefs of societies.... Conservation, rehabilitation and culturally sensitive adaptive re-use of urban, rural and architectural heritage are also in accordance with the sustainable use of natural and human-made resources. Access to culture and the cultural dimension of development is of the utmost importance....[119]

- Governments at the appropriate levels...should identify and document, whenever possible, the historical and cultural significance of areas, sites...and manifestations and establish conservation goals...; (and) promote the awareness of such heritage...and the financial viability of rehabilitation;...local heritage and cultural institutions...and inculcate in children and youth an adequate sense of their heritage...;adequate financial and legal support...; education and training in traditional skills...; the active role of older persons as custodians of cultural heritage;...the social, cultural and economic viability of historically and culturally important sites and communities;...the integrity of the historic urban fabric, and (guide) new construction in historic areas;...adequate legal and financial support..., in particular through adequate training...; incentives...; community-based action...; public and private-sector and community partnerships...; the incorporation of environmental concerns in conservation and rehabilitation projects;...reduced acid rain and other types of environmental pollution that damage buildings...; planning policies, including transport and other infrastructure policies, that avoid environmental degradation of historic and cultural areas; (and) ensure that the accessibility concerns of people with disabilities are incorporated...."[120]

Systematic context

However, these comments for cultural properties were not divorced from any overall strategy for the re-use or rehabilitation of buildings generally. Instead, they are presented against a backdrop of sustainable development in shelter issues generally. The language is equally forthright:

- "We, the States participating in the United Nations Conference on Human Settlements, are committed to...promoting the upgrading of existing housing stock through rehabilitation and maintenance;[121]

- A fundamental principle in formulating a realistic shelter policy is (to) emphasize the increased use and maintenance of existing stock;[122]
- Governments should apply...taxation, monetary and planning policies to stimulate sustainable shelter markets;[123]
- Governments at the appropriate levels should adopt an enabling approach to shelter development, including the renovation, rehabilitation, upgrading and strengthening of the existing housing stock;[124]
- Governments...should adjust legal, financial and regulatory frameworks, including frameworks for contracts, land-use, building codes and standards;[125]
- Government should...improve planning, design, construction, maintenance and rehabilitation;[126]
- To respond effectively to the requirements for...maintenance and rehabilitation of shelter...governments should...facilitate the transfer of planning, design and construction techniques, strengthen the capacities of training institutions and non-governmental organizations to increase and diversify the supply of skilled workers,...promote research, exchange of information and capacity building,...provide training to professionals and practitioners in the construction and development sector to update their skills and knowledge,...support professional groups in offering technical assistance,...revise building codes and regulations...and adopt performance standards as appropriate."[127]

UNESCO
follow-up

It is arguable that the growing influence of this comprehensive approach is also reflected in the new UNESCO program for 1998-1999,[128] which specifies that the integration of heritage within the economic and social life of the community has become a major preoccupation, resulting in a change of emphasis from the protection of monuments *per se* to the revitalization of historic centres, in close liaison with UNESCO's activities for social development.[129]

The more important issue, however, will be to determine how this new thinking will be translated into policies and actions throughout the Member-States.

10. CONCLUSION

An
international
phenomenon

Almost every country on earth has been going through a period of fundamental economic upheaval over the past several years. Although there are differences of degree, no major country has been left untouched. In many places, the change has been a shift from socialist economics to capitalist economics. However, even among countries with traditional western economies, there has been massive re-structuring as countries try to adjust to

New
perceived
demands

- a changing public perception of the role of governments (partly caused by revolutionary changes in "management theory");
- popular insistence on sustainable development and environmental responsibility; and
- an equally popular insistence that it is intrinsically better to be in a proactive mode than a reactive mode.

Primacy of
economics

As the role of the State changes in response to these new perceptions, this combination of factors suggests (at least to some observers) that legislative strategy for the protection of buildings will need to foresee the following basic assumption: far fewer worthy buildings will have their fate in the hands of architects or government officials than in the hands of accountants.

Re-directing
governments

The initial question is how advocates of the protection and rehabilitation of buildings propose to influence government policy in light of this scenario, to ensure that even if governments are not part of the solution, they are at least not part of the problem.

However, that objective is only a beginning; a proper national strategy is capable of doing much more than that. In principle, a carefully prepared and executed national strategy should be capable of allowing any country

Ultimate
objective

- to ensure that over 90 percent of the buildings that it wishes to conserve and rehabilitate are dealt with properly because of the "natural" (but carefully thought-out) forces operating invisibly among property managers (in both the public and private sectors); and
- to require overt State intervention for less than 10 percent (and perhaps even less than 5 percent) of such buildings — i.e., only where unusual circumstances have created a threat that cannot otherwise be properly handled.

Comprehensive
approaches

In short, a carefully prepared national strategy should, in principle, be entirely capable of meeting the goals of housing, heritage and sustainable development simultaneously; furthermore, because of the overlap between many of the objectives of these three policy areas, it may actually be easier for a country to achieve its goals by proceeding on these three fronts jointly, rather than addressing them in isolation from one another.

Next step:
Action

Even though the work of the international community in this area has been fragmented and sometimes uneven, the end result is still a reasonably comprehensive blueprint for national strategies. The challenge is now to translate that blueprint into reality.

ENDNOTES

1 *Agenda 21*, s. 8.7. The full text of Agenda 21 is found in *The Earth Summit*, United Nations, New York, 1993.

2 *Agenda 21*, S. 8.15; see also s. 33.8.

3 The full title is the *Convention for the Protection of Cultural Property in the Event of Armed Conflict*, The Hague, 1954. These conventions and related documents are reproduced in *Conventions and Recommendations of UNESCO Concerning the Protection of the Cultural Heritage*, UNESCO, Paris 1984. The Hague Convention of 1954 is, in several key respects, merely a successor to another convention (also signed at the Hague and called *Hague IV*) entitled *Convention on Laws and Customs of War on Land* (1907); Art.56 of the 1907 convention states that "all seizure of, destruction or wilful damage done to...historic monuments...is forbidden." (This was in turn the direct successor to Art. 56 of a previous convention called *Hague II of 1899*.) These principles, of which the *Hague Convention* of 1954 is the latest articulation, were also enforced at the Nuremburg Trials. The destruction of "cultural monuments" was part of the indictment (s. 8) read at the trials as being "contrary to international conventions...the laws and customs of war, the general principles of criminal law...the internal penal laws of the countries in which such crimes are committed (etc.)." The principal defendant, pertaining to policies of systematic destruction and looting of heritage property, was the Nazi official Alfred Rosenberg; for these and other offences against humanity, Rosenberg was convicted, sentenced and hanged. See *Law, Ethics and the Visual Arts*, by Merryman and Elsen. University of Pennsylvania Press, Philadelphia, 1987.

4 The *Hague Convention* also has the problem of having fewer signatories than the other relevant treaties (the United States and Canada are among many countries that never formally adhered to it).

5 The full title is the *Convention Concerning the Protection of the World Cultural and Natural Heritage*.

6 Article 4.

7 Article 5 (b). To assist in the implementation of this obligation, the Convention specifies a further obligation, at Article 5(e), "To foster the establishment or development of national or regional *centres for training* in the protection, conservation and presentation of the cultural and natural heritage and to encourage scientific research in this field."

8 Article 5(a). Emphasis added.

9 Article 5(a). Emphasis added.

10 Article 1.

11 The Convention also proceeds to establish a committee, which has the further mandate of compiling a World Heritage List. This List does not, of itself, have an intrinsic legal binding effect but can serve useful educational purposes and render certain properties eligible for international financial aid. The List, however, does not (contrary to some lay opinion) constitute the only properties of

"outstanding universal value" targeted by the Convention: see *"Pacta Sunt Servanda"* (by this writer), *Old Cultures in New Worlds*, ICOMOS 8th General Assembly, Symposium Papers, Washington, 1987, Volume 2, p. 869.

12 For example, *Global Strategy for Shelter to the Year 2000*, Resolution 43/181, 1988.

13 For example, the UNCED Resolution of 1989, #44/228.

14 See *Urban Renewal and the Quality of Life*, United Nations, New York, 1980. These symposia were held in 1961, 1970, 1978 and 1979.

15 There were fourteen countries, only one of which was outside Europe.

16 Held in Rio de Janeiro, Brazil, June 3-14, 1992.

17 December 22, 1989, and the outcome was formally adopted by the heads of state (or their representative) of 178 national governments.

18 *Agenda 21*, s. 7.20(b).

19 *Report of Habitat United Nations Conference on Human Settlements*, Vancouver, May 31-June 11, 1976. United Nations, New York, 1976.

20 United Nations Centre for Human Settlements (Habitat), Nairobi, 1990.

21 General Assembly Resolution 43/181.

22 *World Habitat Day, Monday, 3 October 1994*. United Nations Centre for Human Settlements (Habitat), p.3.

23 *Ibid.*

24 S. 28.

25 S. 99.

26 Annex II, s. 12.

27 The verbatim version of the recommendations is found in the compilation, *Conventions and Recommendations of UNESCO etc., op cit.*

28 See *Rules of Procedure Concerning Recommendations to Member States and International Conventions*, under Article IV (par.4) of the UNESCO Constitution. The application to recommendations on the protection of buildings is further described at *Conventions and Recommendations of UNESCO etc., op.cit.*, p. 8.

29 *Ibid.*

30 UNESCO Constitution, Art. 1(b).

31 ICOMOS is a non-governmental organization based in Paris, with a close working relationship with UNESCO pertaining to advice on the drafting of the World Heritage List referred to in footnote 11 above.

32 See *Charters and Conventions*. FHBRO Working Group Guidelines for Significant Interventions, Canadian Parks Service. 2nd Edition. Ottawa, June 1986. *The Venice Charter* spawned a host of imitators. None of these should, however, be confused with legal documents.

33 *Agenda 21*, s. 8.7.

34 *Global Strategy*, ss. 31-32.

35   1972 s.4; 1976 s. 2.

36   *Agenda 21*, s. 8.4(b), and s. 8.12.

37   *Agenda 21*, s. 8.5(a).

38   *Agenda 21*, s. 8.44(a).

39   *Agenda 21*, s. 27.10(a)(ii), and s. 27.10(c).

40   *Agenda 21*, ss. 8.4(d), 8.17, 8.21(c).

41   *Global Strategy*, ss. 26, 38(a), 52.

42   1968 s. 224(b); 1972 s. 8; 1976 S. 9.

43   1972 s. 33; 1976 S. 9.

44   1962 s. 3.

45   1962 s. 33; 1968 s. 20(a).

46   1986 s. 20(a).

47   1976 s. 17(a).

48   1972 s. 34.

49   1962 s. 11.

50   For the reason that many important provisions should optimally be integrated with other legislation, such as land-use planning, environmental controls, etc.

51   1976 s. 13.

52   1968 ss. 21, 22.

53   *Agenda 21*, 1962 s. 23.

54   S. 8.5(b).

55   1972 ss. 32, 34.

56   1976 s. 42.

57   That is why, for example, *Agenda 21* recommends that governments should "remove or reduce those subsidies that do not conform with sustainable development": s. 8.32(b).

58   1976 s. 15.

59   1968 s. 20(b), 20(e); 1976 s. 9.

60   1962 s. 21.

61   1962 s. 17.

62   1962 s. 19.

63   1976 s. 16.

64   1968 s. 25; 1972 s. 45.

65   1962 s. 5, 7(a), 13.

66   1968 s. 8(b).

67   1968 s. 25; 1972 s. 45; 1976 s. 30.

68   1962 s. 22.

69   1968 s. 23, 25.

70   S. 8.21(d).

71   The traditional phrase describing the right of citizens to apply to the courts is "*locus standi*" or "standing." In some countries, the rules concerning "standing" are so restrictive that an individual has no right to be heard by the courts, even when the environmentally damaging activity is flagrantly illegal. In other words, the court refuses to hear the complaint, because it "is none of the plaintiff's business." This is the kind of obstacle that the international declarations have alluded to.

72   1972 s. 44; 1976 s. 12.

73   1962 s. 35; 1972 s. 48; 1976 s. 12.

74   1976 s. 13.

75   1962 s. 27.

76   1976 s. 22.

77   *Agenda 21*, ss. 8.4(c) and s. 8.27, 8.32(c).

78   *Agenda 21*, s. 8.36(a).

79   1968 s. 17(a); 1972 s. 51; 1976 s. 40.

80   1968 s. 16.

81   1968 s. 17(b); 1972 s. 51; 1976 s. 40.

82   1976 s. 44.

83   *Agenda 21*, s. 30.19.

84   *Agenda 21*, s. 8.29.

85   *Global Strategy*, ss. 106-109.

86   *Global Strategy*, s. 67.

87   *Agenda 21*, s. 7.20(e).

88   *Agenda 21*, s. 8.13.

89   *Global Strategy*, s. 15.

90   *Global Strategy for Shelter*, s. 27; also s. 35. This theme is also repeated at several points in Chapter 7 of *Agenda 21*.

91   1976 s. 27.

92   1972 s. 13, 14.

93   1972 s. 38.

94   For example, from owners dissatisfied with the advice or from architects unhappy with the competition.

95   *Agenda 21*, s. 8.41. *Agenda 21* recommends that this be done on the basis of the *SNA Handbook on Integrated Environmental and Economic Accounting*, available from the Statistical Office of the United Nations Secretariat: see s. 8.43(a).

96   *Agenda 21*, s. 8.48(b).

97   1962 s. 34.

98 *Theodosian Code, Majorian Novellae IV*: see *The Theodosian Code*, Clyde Pharr, Trans. Princeton University Press, 1952, 553-4.

99 The *World Heritage Convention* takes a similar position when it declares, at Art. 1, that its focus is on buildings "of outstanding *universal* value." This would convey the impression, to the lay reader, that the pedigree would have to be so staggering that its influence could be felt even on Saturn or Alpha Centauri.

100 The Turkish *Law on Antiquities*. (No. 1710, 25 April 1973).

101 The statute specifies "historic caves, rock shelters, rocks bearing writings and reliefs; mounds, tumuli, sites of ruins; acropolises and necropolises, city walls, castles and towers, all kinds of architectural monuments; theatres, hippodromes, stadia, amphitheatres, agorae and libraries; all kinds of official or private buildings; vestiges of historic roads; bridges, milestones, obelisks, altars, arsenals, quays, aqueducts, cisterns, wells, historic palaces, pavilions, waterside houses, congregational mosques and smaller mosques, open-air oratories; all kinds of pious foundations, fountains, drinking fountains, soup-kitchens, mints, hospitals, mosque clock-rooms, manufactories of silver thread, madrasahs, dervish lodges and hermitages, graveyards, mausolea, mosque cemeteries, tombs, sarcophagi, stelae, vaults, caravanserais, baths, synagogues, basilicae, churches, monasteries and the like, together with collections of buildings made up of several of the aforementioned ... other immovable property together with portions belonging to the aforementioned; remains of ancient monuments and walls, and remnants of scattered bricks and other building-material in an immovable state."

102 Another objective concerning waste, "reduce," is not directly applicable.

103 These "used construction materials" are partly made up of surplus materials from new construction sites (e.g., excess wrapping and waste materials) and partly of materials resulting from demolition work.

104 See, for example, the National Historic Preservation Act of 1966, 16 U.S.C. s. 470 (f) particularly at s. 106.

105 See, for example, the Environment Protection (Impact of Proposals) Act of 1974, or the Australian Heritage Commission Act of 1975, at s. 30.

106 This point was alluded to in *Heritage in the 1990s, op.cit.* It is treated in more detail in "Federal Environmental Impact Assessment and Heritage," *Impact: The Voice of the Canadian Heritage Network.* March 1991, p. 2.

107 There are several relevant publications. See: *Section 4(f) U.S. Federal Highway Administration*, Washington, September 24, 1987; *Section 4(f) Litigation in Which the National Trust Has Participated*, National Trust for Historic Preservation, Washington, 1990; *Highway Litigation under Section 4(f) of the Department of Transportation Act*, National Trust for Historic Preservation, Washington, 1990; *Section 106 Participation by Local Governments*, Advisory Council on Historic Preservation, Washington, 1988; *Section 106 Participation by State Historic Preservation Officers*, Advisory Council on Historic Preservation, Washington, 1988; *Working with Section 106*, Advisory Council on Historic Preservation, Washington, 1986; *A Five-minute Look at Section 106 Review*, Advisory Council on Historic Preservation, Washington, 1989; *Identification of Historic Properties*, Advisory Council on Historic Preservation, Washington, 1988.

108 This approach became fully operational when implementing regulations were passed in 1979.

109 Telephone interview with this writer, August, 1991.

110 *Report of the World Commission on Environment and Development*, 1987.

111 For example, in countries such as Canada, the income tax system was introduced "temporarily" in World War I and again in World War II; the version today stems from the late forties, when certain ideas about urban form prevailed in the circles of power and influence. That mindset was shared by the chief designer of Canada's tax system, Deputy Minister of Finance W.C. Clark, who announced that the entire system of building cities should be scrapped and replaced by a handful of "house factories" modelled precisely on the car industry. This suited the architectural and academic élite, which had announced that pre-existing buildings were "criminal," "pathological" or "perverted" (the principal of McGill University predicted that Canadian cities would be levelled after World War II so that a new generation could start over). Wartime houses were built without basements and furnaces precisely because they were "disposable": they were expected to be destroyed after the war, as soon as the house factories came into production. Although Canada's example was relatively extreme, this was not the only country in which such theories were fashionable at the time.

112 In Canada, for example, "repairs" are tax-deductible for landlords, while "renovations" are not.

113 Heritage Canada is one of many examples.

114 Public Buildings Cooperative Uses Act, 1974, 40 U.S.C. s.606 et seq. Major states in the United States have comparable legislation. See the *Handbook on Historic Preservation Law*, C. J. Duerken, Ed. National Trust and Historic Preservation, Washington, 1983. p. 165.

115 S. 53.

116 *The Habitat Agenda.* s. 27(f)

117 S. 17.

118 S. 49(e)

119 S. 106.

120 SS. 107-8

121 S. 25(f).

122 S. 48.

123 S. 49(d)

124 S. 52 (a)

125 S. 54(b)

126 S. 67(f)

127 S. 69(c), (d), (g), (i), (l), (n).

128 June 14, 1996.

129 S. 65

Other Architecture Books from Dundurn Press ...

Legal and Financial Aspects of Architectural Conservation
Edited by Marc Denhez and Stephen Dennis

A companion volume to *The Heritage Strategy Planning Handbook,* this book is an international study fearuring 18 experts from ten countries describing the legal challenges and solutions relating to the preservation of heritage property. *Legal and Financial Aspects of Architectural Conservation* stems from the conference at Smolenice Castle in Slovakia.

ISBN 1-55002-250-4
216 pages, paperback, $24.99 (US$22.00)

The Canadian Home: From Cave to Electronic Cocoon
by Marc Denhez

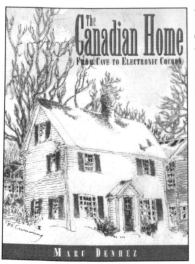

Would you want to live in a factory-molded cube made of plastic, asbestos, and UFFI? With an "H-bomb shelter" and nuclear furnace underneath? Or a house designed by God to harmonize with the cosmic Muzak?

The Canadian Home is a look at how Canadian housing came to be, from primeval origins to the R-2000 house and speculation about habitation in space.

ISBN 1-55002-202-4
350 pages, hardcover, $39.99 (US$35.25)

For Canadian and U.S. orders please call 1(800)565-9523.
For U.K. and European orders please call 01865 750079.

The Canadian Master Architects Series
from Dundurn Press

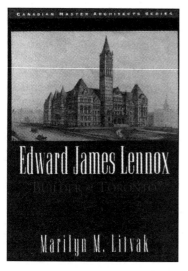

Edward James Lennox: Builder of Toronto
by Marilyn M. Litvak

The first book in the Canadian Master Architects Series, this volume analyzes the life and work of a man who left an indelible mark on the architecture of Toronto. From Old City Hall to Casa Loma, Lennox designed some of the most famous buildings in the city and the country.

ISBN 1-55002-204-0
124 pages, paperback, $19.99 (US$17.50)

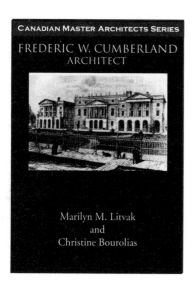

Frederic W. Cumberland
by Marilyn M. Litvak and Christine Bourolias

Like Lennox, F. W. Cumberland helped to build some of Toronto's most memorable structures. Cumberland's work included University College, St. James' Cathedral, and the central section of Osgoode Hall.

ISBN 1-55002-301-2
124 pages, paperback, $19.99 (US$17.50)

For Canadian and U.S. orders please call 1(800)565-9523.
For U.K. and European orders please call 01865 750079.